YOU AREN'T WORTHLESS

Unlock the Truth to Godly Confidence

Kristin N. Spencer

You Aren't Worthless:
Unlock the Truth to Godly Confidence
Copyright © 2019 (Second Edition)
by Kristin Spencer

Cover photography and artwork by: Kristin
Spencer

ISBN-13: 978-1-951040-00-0
ISBN-10: 1-951040-00-7

On The Web
krisitnnspencer.com

Contact the author:
kristin.n.spencer@gmail.com

This book is dedicated to my mother, Peggy Louise. I love you, Mom.

This book is also for any person that has ever felt worthless.
I pray that you would find comfort in the truth of God's word.

TABLE OF CONTENTS

CHAPTER 1

I KNOW HOW YOU FEEL

Have you ever felt worthless? You're not alone. There are so many things in the world around us that tell us that we simply aren't good enough, smart enough, or attractive enough. The world tells us that in order to get rid of our insecurities we need to believe that we are worthy by repeatedly saying we are worthy. But has that actually helped with our insecurities? It has never helped me.

There is a way that you can be delivered from the lie that you are worthless, and the goal of this book is to do just that. *You Aren't Worthless* will walk you through the same healing process that God walked me through over the last fourteen years. Instead of fourteen years, the process described in this book can help you find healing from feelings of worthlessness in just a few days. This book is for anyone who has felt worthless, hurt, and like their life doesn't matter. You do matter, and I will prove that using God's word. On my own journey, I have discovered freedom from low self-esteem, and you can too.

As my husband and I have ministered to others through discipling and counseling over the past seven years, we have seen the negative effects that feelings of worthlessness can cause. Being a foreign missionary also gave me the advantage to see how this isn't just a western problem, but a worldwide, spiritual epidemic.

I have seen the methods I describe in this book bring healing and freedom in Jesus Christ. A Bible-centered approach to dealing with issues of spiritual and physical insecurity creates a strong foundation for healing in this process. We will look at specific examples that draw from characters in God's word that will help us understand how the principles taught in these examples can transform our attitudes about ourselves as individuals, and the reality that is available to us as children of God. I will also dispel popular psychological concepts that the church as a whole has wrongfully embraced as truth.

Gregory Brown, a pastor, professor, and navy reserve chaplain serving at the Handong Global University says, "Kristin exposes the lies of the world system that trap [people] and make them miss the confidence that should come from being Divine image bearers—created to display God's glory. Throughout the rest of the book, she teaches Scriptural truths that bring healing and help foster godly confidence."

I promise that if you follow me through the scriptures with an open heart and a prayerful attitude, you will be set free from the unrealistic expectations that have created your feelings of worthlessness and you will find new fulfillment in the truth that God's love and creative purposes for you make you more valuable than you can imagine.

Please don't wait to embark on your own journey of healing because you think it might be too painful, or that this kind of healing is impossible for you. Be brave and walk with me as we learn about God's plan in creating you, and all of the ways He wants to show you that you aren't worthless. You are very precious in His sight.

LOW CONFIDENCE: THE LOVE AND LIFE STEALER

When you unlock the truth to godly confidence, it will positively improve every aspect of your life. But what if you leave things the way they are now? What risks are you taking? Changing your behavior is difficult, right? What could possibly be worth all of that effort?

First, I want to tell you that it *isn't* that difficult to change your approach to confidence, and you can do so by changing one thing you do every day. Second, you may not realize it, but by settling for a low-confidence attitude, you are missing out on some very important and enjoyable aspects of life in general, but also in your walk with Jesus Christ. But what exactly does the low-confidence life cost you? Here are a few examples.

Greg is in his twenties and even though he would love to have more friends and build a positive support group to counteract his unhealthy family, the thoughts of his mother telling him how hairy and unattractive he is enters his mind every time he thinks about making an

Kristin N. Spencer

effort to get to know someone from work or church better. Why would they want to be friends with him? This low-confidence attitude permeates every aspect of Greg's life. He's miserable and lonely and he doesn't know how to change things.

June loves to write, as long as she doesn't have to deal with any peers. Self-study is the way to go as far as she is concerned. Though she knows she would benefit exponentially from joining a writing group, the idea of being critiqued by more experienced writers is paralyzing. Instead, she refuses to show anyone her writing, hoarding her manuscripts to herself, and improves at a far slower pace than anyone who is willing to reach out for help. She allows her dreams of self-publishing one of her novels to slowly die, a death harkened by her low-confidence approach to life. Her writing goals just aren't worth the risk of letting another person see one of her potential mistakes.

After years of avoiding his calling, Tim has finally given into God and decided to become a pastor. He completes seminary and applies to every church with an opening in his denomination across the country. When he finally gets his dream job, he finds himself miserable. The elders (AKA his bosses) aren't very happy with several things Tim just can't seem to do right. He quits and takes a job at the local bank, where he licks his wounds and decides that maybe he isn't a Christian after all.

What is the dilemma that these three people face? You have probably noticed a theme here: all of their problems can be traced back to their lack of godly confidence. As confidence issues progress, they can also lead to more serious obstacles such as addiction, isolation, and depression. Is there anything in your life that you want to do, but are afraid to pursue due to low confidence? With a little understanding, and a simple, daily practice, you can fully embrace godly confidence and completely transform your life.

When I discovered the truth about godly confidence, every single thing about my approach to life changed. My healthy relationships felt safe and full of love, while I noticed that my unhealthy relationships needed to change. I was finally able to pursue the career of my dreams. All of the bitterness I had been collecting against God changed into love, joy, and confidence in Him. My marriage improved. I became a better mom, daughter, sister, and friend. In addition to all of those awesome transformations, my approach to ministry changed from unsure to dynamic and compassion-driven. I became better at loving people. Does that sound appealing to you?

But before we get to the how, I want to share the why through one last story: my own.

"FOR THE LORD DOES NOT SEE AS MAN SEES; FOR MAN LOOKS AT THE OUTWARD APPEARANCE, BUT THE LORD LOOKS AT THE HEART."
-1 SAMUEL 16:7

Get a head start and download your free pack of printables that accompany this book.
To receive your free printable packet, go to:

youarentworthlessbook.com/packet

Chapter 2

SET FREE

As I watched my daughters play at the park, I looked around and saw the other mothers. I prayed in the quiet spaces of my mind, like usual, and something I will never forget happened. God said something to me that would change my life forever and I pray that it will also change your life. But first, I need to rewind.

GROWING UP IN WESTERN AMERICAN CULTURE

As a young girl, I was very aware of what the world

considered beautiful. This was before people were constantly connected to the internet, but even then there were images taunting me from fashion magazines and television shows. Then there were the living and breathing images of unreachable beauty that I went to school with every day. My family also had a huge role in my understanding of physical beauty. These men and women, who loved Jesus, were often complaining about one body part or another, whether it was their own or that of another person. All of these things pointed to one solution: my physical appearance would never measure up.

As I searched for a group of peers that would accept me, I was usually the willing recipient of cruel jokes and rude comments that turned into mantras I would torture myself with on a daily basis. I sought male affection as a way to battle against these thoughts. I rationalized that if someone wanted to kiss me or have sex with me, then I must be beautiful. But all of these things only left a bigger hole in my heart. I struggled with disordered eating and dressed in oversized clothes.

Once I started walking strongly with the Lord, I thought He would heal all these hurts, but the women I saw at church were struggling with the same insecure feelings as I was. I couldn't see an example of victory anywhere. Although I believed God when I read in His word that He loved me and He created me, somewhere deep inside I clung onto the lie that God had made a mistake. Surely He hadn't planned to make me look this way. Why would He make me like this, and drop me in a world whose standard of beauty would always be out of reach? Other Christians told me that I had low self-esteem, and that I needed to trust God, as if saying those two simple sentences to me would fix all of my problems. I really did not understand God's unconditional love for me, or the fact that God doesn't make mistakes (God cannot lie, Titus 1:2).

In college, I joined the crew team (rowing) and even when I was working out two or three times a day, on a very strict diet as a vegetarian, I was still a size 10. God did not make me to be thin. That is something I accept now, but then I was extremely irritated by the entire situation. I got involved at church and kept quiet about my confidence problems. My insecurity was like a festering wound that I felt all the time. The deep ache permeated every part of my being. And I noticed that other people in the church, both men and women, said demeaning things about their own physical appearances. When they discussed being thankful, it was always about things or spiritual gifts. I don't remember ever hearing anyone say that we should be thankful for the body God had given us. I kept seeing people couple up and get married, but no one ever seemed interested in me romantically. This only encouraged my belief in the lie that no one could or would ever think I was beautiful. Looking back I can see that God was protecting me until I met my husband.

MARRIAGE DIDN'T FIX ME

Even after I got married, though, I still felt unworthy and ugly. My husband struggled with a pornography addiction, and that only magnified my own insecurities. Instead of encouraging him that he could overcome his addictions, I shrunk back, believing in my heart that I could never live up to the perfect images of naked women he could find online. My heart was broken into so many pieces. I was pregnant with our first child, a girl, and I was afraid that I would never be able to be a positive influence in her life. After 20 hours of hard labor, she was born by emergency C-section. This was another strike against my already less-than-perfect body since I ended up suffering from diastasis recti (abdominal separation) that made me look like I was continually three months pregnant. I struggled with postpartum depression and spent many afternoons planning my own suicide. My idea was to wait until I had stored enough breast milk to last my daughter for a few months.

I was under a deep deception about God's love for me, and this trickery drained the joy out of every positive thing in my life. I was desperate for some kind of change, but I didn't know what to do. At this point my husband was still struggling with his addiction and was working two jobs. He lost interest in going to church, so I would go with my daughter and sit alone during most services in the nursing mothers' room. It was one of the loneliest times in my life.

Eventually, God delivered my husband from his pornography addiction, and he cultivated a more intimate relationship with the Lord. He went back to church, and we met other Christian families who we could be ourselves with. A home fellowship formed, and along with it came much needed encouragement and fruitfulness. My insecurities seemed to fade into the background as God called my husband and me to the mission field. I was pregnant with our second daughter and had her just a few weeks before we moved to Hungary to attend the School of Missions at Calvary Chapel Bible College, Europe.

There, for the first time in my life, I met men and women who had strong, godly confidence. I could see that many of the staff members had victory and trusted in God's love for them. I still didn't know how to find that peace and trust in God with regards to the person He'd made me to be, but at least I knew it was possible. Since I had a newborn at that time, I spent a lot of time alone in our family's living area. But I watched how the others interacted with and loved each other. We had women's prayer once a week, and that was a lifeline. I also attended the Missions class taught by a godly woman who would end up being a loving example of godly confidence in my life. It was a time when God built me up for the next battle, which I never imagined would take place the way it did.

NEW DREAMS, REPEATED DEFEATS

At the end of Bible college my husband and I felt that God had called us to move to Greece, a European country on the coast of the Aegean Sea. Once we moved, we began to serve with another couple who had more experience as missionaries. But the struggles I had with my own insecurities were magnified under the lens of one of the people we served with. The wife of this older couple constantly questioned my ability to do things God had entrusted me with, including being a godly mother. I was repeatedly told by both members of the older couple that as soon as a real worship leader could be found, I would no longer be leading worship. There were also subtle negative comments about my weight and ability to learn a new language. I was told that I didn't know as much about things as I let on, and that I was too vague when it came to telling other people details about my life.

Previous bad habits crept back in as I allowed others to make rude comments about me, and most of the time I agreed with them. How could more mature Christians be wrong? Slowly, these people also chipped away at the security I had in my friendships with other Christians. I felt alone. The breaking point came when the people we ministered to started coming to me to encourage me to talk to the other people about the rude things they frequently said to and about me in group settings. These Greek brothers and sisters in the faith were offended on my behalf and started vocally supporting me and encouraging me by saying that God was using me positively in their lives. After prayerful consideration and an attempt to follow the model we find for dealing with conflict in Matthew 18, I tried to talk to these people about what had happened. A few meetings later, I was accused of being too sensitive. There were other factors as well, but, after a time of prayer and fasting, my husband decided it was God's will that we distance ourselves from this destructive situation. I was six months pregnant with our third child at the time (an amazing little boy).

BACK AT THE PARK

It was soon after these events took place that I was at the park, watching the girls play, with an obtrusive pregnant belly. I prayed about my broken heart and my confusion about the way God had made me. I remember asking God, "If you wanted me to be able to minister to people, why did you make me like this?" and instead of saying anything, God gave me a vision I would never forget. But more on that later.

After that, I heard a voice tell me that my low self-esteem was a type of pride—a sinful behavior that was keeping me far from the Lord. I remember what it was like to see this pride in my heart for the first time. I was so disgusted that I wanted to vomit. I prayed and asked God for forgiveness, and since that moment I have been free from the prison of insecurities I had built around myself. I have still been tempted to go back to that sin, like a dog returning to its own vomit (Proverbs 26:11), but thankfully God has given me victory to resist this temptation. Since then, I have been able to accept God at His word, and embrace His promises for me and my life as His child.

I have learned so much about God and His love for me through this process, and I want to help you understand His love for you as well. Maybe you feel like you are walking around with an open wound and no one will talk about it. That is why God put it on my heart to write this book, because the enemy knows and exploits a particular weakness that none of us will talk about. I am putting an end to that right now. Let's talk about it. Let's talk until every Christian on this planet understands God's love and plans for them.

CHAPTER 3

TWO POWERFUL LIES CHRISTIANS BELIEVE

You live in the world, so you already know about the torrent of lies that flows out of the entertainment industry, advertising agencies, and is even perpetuated by the church. I am a Los Angeles, California girl. In Southern California, the idea that permeates the lifestyle is that all women should have large breasts, small waist lines, and wear makeup. Oh yeah, and they'd better look perfect in a bathing suit, because everyone lives at the beach in summer. These days, the expectations for men are equally unrealistic. They are expected to live at the gym, have chiseled everything, and be completely hairless.

When I was younger, I had never found anyone openly proclaiming that all these ideas have no biblical basis among my family of other believers. I heard that inner beauty should be emphasized above all else, over and over again, but no one said anything to directly contradict the unrealistic expectations associated with physical appearance within the culture surrounding me. I wanted to be told that I was attractive, both inside and out. I looked around and could see that others were craving the same thing, but never found assurance of that fact, even within the church amongst other believers.

While I agree that inner beauty—beauty perpetuated by our desires to follow Jesus Christ and be more like Him—is very important, at the same time, it is foolish to ignore our physical insecurities. As a church body, we must acknowledge God's perfect and creative plan for our personalities as well as our physical bodies.

For this reason, I believe that within the church we should make a point to tell others that they are attractive when it is appropriate. I am not saying that men should go around the church telling every woman she is beautiful, because some women might get the wrong idea. But we need to tell our daughters. Sisters need to tell sisters. Fathers need to tell their sons that they are handsome, and purposefully created. Brothers need to encourage each other in this way.

I remember when my husband and I were getting ready to graduate from the Missions program at Calvary Chapel Bible College Europe. My father-in-law came to watch our graduation, and took us out to buy dress clothes for the occasion—we had forgotten about graduation when we packed for our family of four, nine months earlier. I remember one of the pastors looked at me in my new dress, and told me how beautiful I looked. It wasn't awkward or inappropriate. In fact my husband was right there. It was an older brother (in the Lord) moment, and it made me feel so special and cherished. If we want to defend against Satan's lies, we need to battle them with truth. God only makes exquisite creations, including His children.

THE NEWEST FAD

If we look at the way physical attractiveness has manifested through history, we see that what is considered gorgeous is not a static thing. It changes depending on popular culture over time. I always hear robust women, like me, lamenting over the renaissance age because full-figured women were considered to be the ultimate beauties. In fact, if you look at artwork during that time, some of women are painted to appear pregnant. This ideal of beauty had to do with procreation, and women with wider hips and larger breasts were believed to be more successful in duties such as childbearing and breast feeding, although now we know this is belief is unfounded. According to my Art History professor in university, strange ideals of beauty have affected art since art began. I'll take her word for it.

We have all heard that during the Golden Age of Hollywood in the 1950s, women like Marilyn Monroe were popularizing the full-figured look. Men who were "rough around the edges" were considered to be the most handome, with actors like Humphrey Bogart and James Cagney (they are both on IMDB's list of Greatest Tough Guy Actors) gaining a majority of the attention. Then, in the mid 1960s we had the popularity of ultra thin models, like Twiggy. As someone who sews clothes, it makes sense to me that fashion designers want to use thin models, because it is much easier to sew couture clothes for women with fewer curves to account for. But that one fact does not mean that thin is the only kind of beautiful. So we see that over time, the standard of attractiveness has constantly changed.

The idea that women should be as thin as possible, while retaining curves in particular places, has been mainstream for many years. Once in a while, the media will pick an exception to this rule, like Jennifer Lopez, Beyoncé, or Kim Kardashian, but these are still preconceived molds hardly any of us can fit into. Men are pressured to look like one of the Hemsworth brothers with chiseled features and perfectly symmetrical faces. In fact, we use these preconceived ideas to measure the value of others. We look at a man or woman and make a decision about how pleasing they are. If they are more attractive than we are, we envy them and assume they must feel confident about how they look. If we think they are less attractive than we are, we may be tempted to think of them when we attempt to make ourselves feel better about our own lack of attractiveness. Either way. this is a very dangerous game and it is also sinful behavior. Even people who fit into the mold of what the world considers to be beautiful will feel insecure and empty without Jesus Christ. We all have insecurities that Satan wants to exploit.

From a business perspective, it is extremely profitable to exploit people's insecurities. If you look at the magazine section of the grocery store, what will you see? Hundreds of images of men and women that are aimed at making you feel worse about yourself. But why? Well, if they can offer you some tips or tricks to make you look like the photoshopped images of perfection on the cover, they can sell you their magazine, and various other products that you don't actually need. There is greed involved on the part of the magazine makers, and their ultimate goal is to create discontentment in you. The less content you are with how you look and what you have (materialism), the more they can sell you. This is a continual cycle that results in multiplied profits for the magazines and their advertisers, while on a personal level it is a destructive pattern in your life that makes you less able to share the love of Jesus Christ with others. It is a complex web of deception that feeds many different types of sin, and steals joy from every person that is trapped in it.

Popular culture, and unfortunately Western Christian culture as well, perpetuate two very significant lies that Satan wants us to believe. These two lies completely devastate us and render us useless as soldiers in God's army. Let's examine them each on their own.

LIE #1: GOD MADE A MISTAKE WHEN HE CREATED YOU

Do you really believe that God had a plan when He created you, or do you think that God made some mistake? Maybe you don't like the way your hair frizzes when it's humid outside. Maybe you hate the way your elbows look. There are literally hundreds of things you could pick to dislike about your physical body. For me, my weight was always the problem. As soon as I went through puberty, I had to work very hard to be thin, and no matter how hard I worked at it, I failed. I remember my mom telling me that once she went through puberty she had to be very careful about what she ate to maintain her weight, and I followed suit. I limited my calories and exercised excessively. In a world that felt so out of my control, disordered eating gave me a sense of control I had never experienced before. I knew that my parents loved me, but my parents' insecurities further communicated to me that if I wanted to be considered beautiful, I would have to attempt to meet the worldly expectation of beauty. I honestly cannot remember anyone in my family telling me that I was beautiful, except for a few occasions when I dressed up for a school dance or a special occasion. This only reinforced the idea in my mind that I was only good-looking when I tried really hard.

At this point, I knew about God. Even when my parents no longer took us to church, my grandmother would make sure to pick me up and take me if I said I wanted to go. But I felt betrayed by God. If He loved me and had a special plan for my life, why had He made me fat and worthless in the eyes of everyone else? It didn't make sense to me. It seemed like no matter what I did, I was a failure. I never really excelled in one specific area, as I was never the smartest or most athletic person. It also seemed I was lacking in the looks department because I never saw any evidence that I was physically desirable. I knew Bible verses that were supposed to help me, but I didn't believe them. I refused to believe that God had a specific plan and person in mind when He created me.

Satan does not always need to tell us lies to succeed; sometimes he just needs to make us doubt. That was the case in my life. It started with a quiet question in my mind, "Did God really create you this way?" I allowed my own unreal expectations for my life to create distance between God and me. God's plan for my life should have meant that I got all of the things the world said I should want, right? Eventually, I started to believe that God had made a mistake when He created me. I believed Satan over God. I gave into the same temptation that Eve did in the Garden of Eden at the beginning of time.

But Jesus

I thought if I were really part of God's awesome plan, I should be beautiful, popular, and have a good family life. I chose to ignore scriptures like John 15:20, *"Remember the word that I said to you, 'A servant is not greater than his master.' If they persecuted Me, they will also persecute you. If they kept My word, they will keep yours also."* The second half of the verse talks about how they kept track of what Jesus said to try to catch Him in a trap. The life of a Christ-follower is supposed to be closely aligned with Christ. Last time I checked, Jesus wasn't popular, extremely handsome, or immediately successful at getting all of His family to believe He was actually God. People constantly tried to catch Him doing something wrong so they could accuse him of breaking Jewish law and get rid of Him (John 10:33). The Bible says that there was nothing special about how He looked (Isaiah 53:2). For a time His own brothers thought He was lying about being the Messiah (John 7:5).

Was Jesus living according to God's plan? Yes! Did Jesus have all the things the world tells us we should have? Absolutely not. One of the reasons it is so easy to believe that God made a mistake when He created us is because we do not seek God's will for our lives. If seeking to be within the confines of God's will was our main priority in life, our ability to adhere to the culturally accepted physical standards of physical attractiveness would not be so important. But we all know that if we expect to have worldly success, we need to look the part, whatever that means. If we would trust God to place us where we should be, and help us to achieve His plans for our lives, we would not feel the need to propel ourselves forward in our personal lives or careers. We would be satisfied where we are right now, in Jesus.

✿ ✿ ✿

LIE #2: YOU WILL NEVER BE WORTHY OF LOVE UNLESS YOU CONFORM TO THE WORLD'S STANDARDS OF BEAUTY

Every single person on Earth experiences the all-consuming desire to feel loved. It is something that is inherently built into our make up as humans. The reason we desire this is because our God is a God of emotions, and we are made in His image (Genesis 1:27). God also built this desire into us because He wants to fulfill it with His perfect love for us (1 John 4:18) via a fulfilling relationship with Himself. Unfortunately, many times we either do not know about God's love for us, or we refuse to accept it. This leaves us with broken hearts, yearning to feel loved and accepted. In our attempts to satisfy this longing for love and relationship, we strike out on our own in a broken world, searching for perfect love that simply does not exist apart from God.

Maybe you're in the group of followers of Jesus Christ who know about God's love for them but are choosing not to believe. I can relate because that is the path that I chose for too many years. When I was a teenager, I didn't feel loved by my parents. That might sound a bit harsh, but in all actuality, not even a parent can fill the love gap in your heart that only God is big enough to fill. I don't blame them. A majority of the problems I had were due to my own refusal to acknowledge God's love. My response to the emotions that resulted from my lack of understanding of God's love for me was to try to find some other kind of love to fill the emptiness in my heart. I thought romantic love would do the trick

—that if I could convince someone to love me, in spite of my less-than-acceptable physical appearance, I would feel better. I was wrong.

According to the way romantic love works in the world between a man and a woman, you have to find someone that finds you attractive. That means you need to look and act a certain way. You should aspire to make yourself as physically attractive as possible. Your company must be enjoyable. It means that you have to throw away anything the Bible says about premarital sex, or sexual purity. If you expect someone to attempt to love you, you have to be willing to give them what they want. Men are taught, from a very young age, that they should want sex with anyone who will give it to them. Men are also taught that pornography is a normal thing. In response to this, women are taught that it is normal for men to expect abnormally-proportioned women who will do whatever they are told to do, in order to bring about the physical satisfaction of their partner. Recently, women have also begun to take a more active role in the use of pornography. It is no wonder that this leads to all kinds of sexual impurity, brokenness, and addiction. This is not the same kind of deep, selfless, soul-bonding sexual intimacy that God created to happen between a husband and wife. Nor is marital love a replacement for the love of our infinite Creator, even in the best, most godly marriages.

Ladies and gentlemen, we have been doing ourselves a great disservice. Why would we settle for the world's empty imitation of God's love? We choose to believe the lie that the only way to fill the need for love in our lives is to do whatever it takes to earn reciprocal human affection. Satan arrogantly throws it in our faces that God doesn't really love us the way He says He does. These are just a few of Satan's lies:

If God really loved me...

He would not have created illness.

He would not have allowed my parents to neglect loving me the way I needed to be loved.
He would have never let that horrible thing happen to me.
He would have given me the things I wanted in life.
He would have brought me the perfect spouse.
He would have given me perfect friends.
He would have stopped people from being mean to me and hurting me over and over.
He would have made people appreciate me for who I am.

The list goes on.

These thoughts do not lead to healing; they lead to dangerous assumptions about God. Satan is twisting the truth, because he wants you to believe that God allows evil and injustice to exist in the world because God does not love you. God gives every person a choice about how he or she will live their life. When people choose sin and defeat over repentance and victory, it affects the people around them, including you and me. Sin is really what causes the hurts in our lives. God longs to help us through these hurts, and assures us that His love is enough to counteract all of them. But if you are anything like I was, you refuse to believe God, because that means you have to trust Him and allow Him to be in complete control of your life. If you expect God to act as a magic genie granting all of your wishes, you misunderstand who God is. He does not function that way. His plan is perfect, and He only wants the best for us, even when that means we will experience suffering.

I had gotten into the dangerous habit of refusing to trust God. When He tried to show me His love for me, I rejected His truth. Satan was winning, and I had become a useless Christian. I couldn't point anyone else toward victory in Jesus because I wasn't living in it myself.

I sought out physical and romantic intimacy as a teenager. My boyfriend was as attentive as any non-Christian 16-year-old boy could be. I thought that if we had sex, the giant hole in my heart would be full, but instead, I felt more empty than ever. And then, after a year and a half of being in an exclusive relationship, he broke up with me over the phone.

I cried into the wireless receiver. "You said you loved me! Did that change overnight? I don't understand."

His response was short and lacked any emotion, "It isn't all about you."

Click.

Not even his friends had expected that to happen. I certainly hadn't seen it coming. I was heartbroken and angry. But underneath all of those feelings, I understood that God was reaching toward me. He was waiting to help me through my life, if I would just trust and believe Him. My Heavenly Father tried to help me understand His unconditional love. He desired to save me from the emptiness I had felt so trapped by. I still wasn't ready to listen.

WHEN WE DON'T BELIEVE GOD'S WORD

The first lie we looked at tells us that when God made us, He made a mistake. In the same vein, the second lie tells us that unless we look a certain way, we will never be worthy of love. The reason both of these lies are so destructive and create so many problems in our relationships with God is that they attempt to convince us that God's word doesn't mean what it says. That is a huge problem, because when we try to separate God's word from God Himself, we create an idol. We take God and try to make Him line up with our opinion of who He should be, even if these opinions are contrary to His Word, the Bible. If we take God and give Him our own list of characteristics, He isn't God anymore. We have made our own *false* god to worship.

CHAPTER 4

THE DECEPTION OF PRIDE VS. THE HONESTY OF HUMILITY

Pride is such a dangerous thing because it keeps us blind toward our true identity in Jesus Christ. Jesus was the most humble human being ever to walk the Earth. As a human form of God, He took on the punishment for all of our sins. If we hope to live a liberated and fruitful life, we need to become more like Jesus, and less like ourselves. In John 3:30, John the Baptist says, *"He must increase, but I must decrease."* If we want to be more like Jesus, pride is not the way to get there.

If you are anything like me, you may think, "Why are you talking about pride? I thought this book was to help people that need to increase their confidence. I have low self-esteem. I don't even like me, so how can I be prideful?" Those are valid questions, and I promise I will answer them if you continue reading. This chapter will deal with pride and humility, concepts that are mentioned in the Bible. The next chapter will address popular confidence concepts that the Bible does not mention. Let's get started.

CONFIDENCE CONCEPTS THAT ARE MENTIONED IN THE BIBLE

The Bible is full of amazing wisdom. In it, we see many stories that show us what consequences will follow our disobedience to God. The goal of this section is to discuss two biblical principles that shape whether we will live our lives following after our own desires and thoughts, or trying to be like Jesus. Pride and humility are very important concepts in the Bible and in our lives as followers of Jesus Christ.

THE DECEPTION OF PRIDE

"Pride goes before destruction, and a haughty spirit before a fall." -Proverbs 16:18

The first concept we'll look at is pride. The Bible actually has a lot to say about this one word. The English language is ambivalent sometimes; therefore, we use the words "pride" and "proud" interchangeably. However, I would like to distinguish between the two, because as you are about to see, in the Bible, pride is a sinful behavior. At the same time, I want to be able to encourage my kids by telling them how proud I am of them for the various ways they behave and the positive things they pursue. I tell them that I'm proud of them, and then I explain that I rejoice over their efforts to do their best and to do the things they know Jesus wants them to do. This is not the same kind of pride we are talking about in this section. Instead, we will be discussing personal pride. We will be using the Dictionary's most basic definition of "pride."

"Pride is the quality or state of being proud; inordinate self-esteem; an unreasonable conceit of one's own superiority in talents, beauty, wealth, rank, etc., which manifests itself in lofty airs, distance, reserve, and often in contempt of others" [1].

If we take that definition and boil it down to its concentrated parts we can use a more simple description: the pride described here is equivalent to self-love.

In the Bible we see the word "pride" over and over— it is discussed a lot. Usually when we see the word "pride" in God's word, it discusses a punishment because of it, or a bad situation related to it. Pride is not presented as a positive concept in the Bible, and we soon learn that God is always against man's pride. "Pride" is mentioned 51 times in the NKJV Bible and "proud" is mentioned 47 times. In each of these 98 mentions, it always has a negative connotation. It is never once mentioned as a positive thing. In fact, we often see it in contrast to humility, which we will talk about in the next section of this chapter. Pride and humility are opposite concepts: keep that in mind.

On one side of the coin, we have the world telling us that we deserve respect. From the world's perspective, pride is a valuable concept. If we take pride in our work, we attach our personal values to it, and that is considered good. If we make our mothers proud, that means that they can find value in what a good job they did raising us. Racial pride means that we are proud of where our ancestors came from—we attach our positive feelings about ourselves to our ethnicity. These ideas seem positive when we look at them without the biblical attitude toward pride. "You should respect me because I do good work, I am a worthy individual in the eyes of my parents, and I am [insert race here]." On the other side of the coin, when we look at the Bible, we see a very different picture.

Let's take a look at some verses that describe pride and its consequences.

"For all that is in the world—the lust of the flesh, the lust of the eyes, and the pride of life—is not of the Father but is of the world." -1 John 2:16

"When pride comes, then comes shame; but with the humble is wisdom." -Proverbs 11:2

"By pride comes nothing but strife, but with the well-advised is wisdom." -Proverbs 13:10

"In the mouth of a fool is a rod of pride, but the lips of the wise will preserve them." -Proverbs 14:3

"Everyone proud in heart is an abomination to the Lord; Though they join forces, none will go unpunished." -Proverbs 16:5

"Pride goes before destruction, and a haughty spirit before a fall." -Proverbs 16:18

"A man's pride will bring him low, but the humble in spirit will retain honor." -Proverbs 29:23

"... lest being puffed up with pride he fall into the same condemnation as the devil." -1 Timothy 3:6

When we look at all of these different verses, we can create a new, biblical definition of pride. According to the Bible, pride is actually the belief that we know better than or are higher than others, including God.

Yikes! That sentence should give us the shivers because we are instructed to fear God, and we should not allow our deceitful hearts trick us into feeling that we know better than He does.

If we look in a lexicon, we will see that the words that are translated into pride from the Greek and Hebrew can also be translated as arrogant or high-minded. Has there ever been someone in your life that thinks they are the smartest, most correct person out of anyone they know? When we think of people that possess these qualities, are our thoughts about them positive, or negative? Usually, when I see someone who believes that pride is the most important human characteristic, the next thought that enters my head is, "egotistical jerk." Obviously, that is not very Christ-like of me, and I need to repent and ask God to help me love them with an unconditional love. But pride is not only offensive to God—it exasperates our human flesh as well. We do not like other people's pride, but we certainly enjoy feeling prideful ourselves. That is the way Satan wants it, because then we compete with each other. To think that I am better and deserve more respect than others is a slippery slope toward feeling superior to God. That is the same way that Satan himself fell.

"How you are fallen from heaven, O Lucifer, son of the morning! How you are cut down to the ground, You who weakened the nations! For you have said in your heart: 'I will ascend into heaven, I will exalt my throne above the stars of God; I will also sit on the mount of the congregation on the farthest sides of the north; I will ascend above the heights of the clouds, I will be like the Most High.'" -Isaiah 14:12-14

That is what pride does. It tells us that we know better than God, we don't need God, we can do things on our own, and our opinions matter more than God's. This is the same behavior that got Satan and one third of all the angels kicked out of heaven. We need to take these warnings about pride very seriously because pride has severe consequences.

These ideas remind me of the things we discussed in the previous chapter. Do you remember my talking about how I did not trust God because He did not do the things I thought He should? I wanted to fit into the world's opinion of beauty, have a great family life, and be well liked by a lot of different people. I did not like that God wouldn't give me these things. In my heart, I told God I knew better than Him. My attitude was prideful! I was guilty of the sinful behavior of pride.

By this point, I hope you are starting to wonder if you are guilty of the sin of pride as well. How can you tell? Pride can easily sneak into your life unannounced. So here are a few questions you can ask yourself to help you determine if you have also fallen into the sinful temptation of pride.

-Is there any area of my life that I am unsatisfied in? Does this dissatisfaction come because I am disappointed by the sins of someone else, or because I feel like I don't have what I deserve?
-Do I feel bad about myself? Why? Because I don't live up to God's righteous standards (I am feeling convicted by the Holy Spirit), or because I do not get the assurance from other people that I feel I need?
-Do I accept the person God has made me? Why or why not?
-Am I angry about the way my life is going? Have I been feeling angry toward God lately?
-Do I pray, "It isn't fair, God," or other similar prayers?

-Do I think that my way is better than God's way? (This was one of ancient Israel's biggest problems.)

Physical Evidence: Time and Money

Another way to determine if we are struggling with pride is to think about how we spend our time and money. We tend to spend more time and money on things that are more important to us.

How much time do I spend on my hair and clothes? How much money do I spend on makeup and haircuts? I am not saying it is wrong to care about your appearance. Whenever I go out on a date with my husband, my kids know I will spend an extra 15 minutes on hair and makeup (which I rarely wear), because I want to make my husband feel special. I will also wear something more dressy than my usual jeans, t-shirt, and girly cardigan combination. I want him to know I care about him, and spending a little extra time on my appearance is just one of many ways I can do that.

The way we distribute time and money can always be used to measure our true motivations. Why am I dressing up? Is it to show my husband that I care about him, or to get attention from other men? Another motivation may be deference. In many cultures the way you dress communicates your respect and appreciation for the hosts, and I do not want to offend anyone by dressing too casually. But if my motivation is to make myself more physically attractive so I will get more attention, then it is sinful. This is an attempt to feel more important based on other people's reactions to my physical appearance. The goal is to inflate my personal pride.

The Bible tells us that we should not devote our focus solely to our appearance. We have to go one step further.

Kristin N. Spencer

"Do not let your adornment be merely outward—arranging the hair, wearing gold, or putting on fine apparel —rather let it be the hidden person of the heart, with the incorruptible beauty of a gentle and quiet spirit, which is very precious in the sight of God." -1 Peter 3:1-3

Most people reference this verse as belonging only to women since it was written directly to women, but the biblical principles can apply to anyone. Are men able to focus on their apparel? Yes, but instead they also can endeavor to have a gentle and quiet spirit (the complicated dynamic between husbands and wives in 1 Peter 3 is explained in detail by Travis and me in our book *Holy Sex Reboot: My Sexual Identity in Christ*). Do you spend as much time beautifying your inner person by studying God's word as you do on your outward appearance? If not, I want to encourage you to take time to pray about whether the way you spend your time and money points to the sin of pride.

Prideful Thoughts

There are many ways that pride affects us in everyday life. It does more than make us consider how we dress. It can manifest itself in the ways we speak, act, and most importantly, think. No one else may know the prideful thoughts that one allows to happen in the recesses of one's heart, but God does. In 1 Samuel 16:7 it says, *"For the Lord does not see as man sees; for man looks at the outward appearance, but the Lord looks at the heart."*

Do you ever have prideful thoughts? Sometimes I think things like, "They should have asked me to do that, I'm better at it than her." Ouch! That is pride, and if it is left unchecked, it can turn into the life-devouring beast called bitterness.

Now that we understand how God feels about the sin of personal pride and how catastrophic it is, we need to look closely into its counterpart, humility.

THE HONESTY OF HUMILITY

"Remind them to be subject to rulers and authorities, to obey, to be ready for every good work, to speak evil of no one, to be peaceable, gentle, showing all humility to all men." -Titus 3:1-2

Humility is an important concept because it helps us guard against bitterness in our hearts, it gives us the correct outlook in relation to God and others, and it is one of the characteristics that sets us apart as different from the world. One of the verses from the Old Testament that we see the apostles quoting several times in the New Testament is Proverbs 3:34, *"God resists the proud, but gives grace to the humble."* It seems like wherever pride is, humility is there, also.

When we give up pride, we are told we should embrace humility. This is the pattern that the Bible gives us to show us how to combat pride. As a young Christian, I kept hearing the same message over and over again—"We need to be humble, not with false humility, but sincere humility." I was so confused by this. Why were people always talking about humility this way? It seemed like a mystery I would never solve. How could I be humble, without having false humility, when I could not figure out what it meant to be truly humble? Maybe I am the only one who struggled with this, but I could not figure out this biblical concept. I saw biblical examples of humility, mainly in Jesus Christ, but I did not understand how the concept applied to *my* life.

If we closely examine biblical examples and definitions, we will see that humility always means that we are to look at others as more important than ourselves. In Strong's Concordance, one of the definitions of the Greek word for humility is, "a deep sense of one's (moral) littleness" [2]. Notice that it does not say worthlessness, which I think is the definition a lot of us associate with humility. Being humble has nothing to do with feeling worthless. If we look at our Heavenly Father, the true meaning of humility becomes much clearer.

The more time I spend with God, the more I understand that He knows so much (He knows everything), and I do not. I begin to understand that compared to God, I am little. I do not know anything. When I think about the face of our Creator, I start to understand humility. God is big and scary. This fact makes me very thankful that He loves me and wants to have a relationship with me. I would not want to face God as an enemy. I would lose. I would die.

We see this principle in scripture as well, *"The fear of the Lord is the instruction of wisdom, and before honor is humility."* –Proverbs 15:33

Let's take this opportunity to see what else the Bible has to say about humility and the humble.

"The humble He guides in justice, and the humble He teaches His way." –Psalm 25:9

"My soul shall make its boast in the Lord; the humble shall hear of it and be glad." –Psalm 34:2

"When pride comes, then comes shame; but with the humble is wisdom." –Proverbs 11:2

"A man's pride will bring him low, but the humble in spirit will retain honor." –Proverbs 29:23

"Likewise you younger people, submit yourselves to your elders. Yes, all of you be submissive to one another, and be clothed with humility, for 'God resists the proud, but gives grace to the humble.'" –1 Peter 5:5

"But avoid foolish and ignorant disputes, knowing that they generate strife. And a servant of the Lord must not quarrel but be gentle to all, able to teach, patient, in humility correcting those who are in opposition, if God perhaps will

grant them repentance, so that they may know the truth, and that they may come to their senses and escape the snare of the devil, having been taken captive by him to do his will." -2 Timothy 2:23-26

Throughout these verses we see that the humble will be able to learn from God and that God will give wisdom to those with humble hearts. These things are in stark contrast to pride. In almost every verse, we see that God will resist the proud, pride is shameful, and pride will always bring us lower.

In my quest to understand humility, these verses started to create a picture for me of how I wanted to be, but I still did not understand how to be sincerely humble. Then I had a breakthrough.

I Want That

When my husband and I were going through the Missions School in Bible college, something amazing happened. I met real-life, humble Christians. I had met humble Christians before, but I had not been able to recognize their humility. For the first time in my life, I was able to distinguish between humble behavior and prideful behavior. I noticed that these humble brothers and sisters all shared similar attitudes about advising others. When it came to the Bible, they were bold and confident. When it came to people's personal matters, they were quiet, unless asked. Even when someone would ask them for advice about something, they would gently give their opinion in a way that would make the recipient feel loved instead of condemned.

I would watch them when other people acknowledged their personal accomplishments. I always saw the same thing on their faces, sincere embarrassment, every single time. They were uncomfortable with any praise that may have been directed at them instead of God. When there was a disagreement about something, they were always calm, not insisting the other person agree with their position. Once I realized what true humility was, I wanted it. I wanted to be as close to God as I could see they were. I wanted the quiet confidence in God that they had. I was hooked.

Little did I know, I was about to get a lesson in what humility was not. Since I was starting to recognize humility in people, it also became more obvious when people were operating out of pride. I started to recognize the false humility I had been previously warned about. My new struggle became, how can I respond to their pride with personal humility? In chapter one, I mention that I had a problem with feeling worthless. I wasn't getting the attention or recognition I thought I deserved from others. Sadly, because of those sinful thoughts, I had set myself up to accept quite the opposite when I discovered the true meaning of humility. In my lack of experience, I assumed that if someone wanted to violate my personal boundaries (which I didn't really have at the time) and tell me how awful I was, I should let them.

Stop Tolerating Sin, Kristin

Previously, I mentioned an incident that caused me personal pain and spiritual growth. The couple who led our ministry that I served under on my first mission were constantly bringing up their opinions of my shortcomings in front of the people to whom we were ministering. They would argue with me about almost anything I said and they questioned my ability to accurately share stories from my past. Some of the believers we ministered to came to me and insisted that I do something. They said I was passively letting the other people engage in sinful activity against me.

Of course, my brothers and sisters in the Lord were right; I had not responded to any of the accusations that were made against me. Instead, I started to believe them all. At first, I attempted to change my personality to accommodate the leadership's desires. When that did not work, I quietly refused to talk or share any of my opinions. But the situation kept getting worse. At the time, my husband helped me realize that I should confront the leadership, according to the model we see in Matthew 18:15-17, and try to help them see that they had sinned against me by slandering my character.

"Moreover if your brother sins against you, go and tell him his fault between you and him alone. If he hears you, you have gained your brother. But if he will not hear, take with you one or two more, that 'by the mouth of two or three witnesses every word may be established.' And if he refuses to hear them, tell it to the church. But if he refuses even to hear the church, let him be to you like a heathen and a tax collector." -Matthew 18:15-17

After several unsuccessful conversations between them and me, my husband insisted on being there with me in pursuit of a more balanced discussion. With Travis holding my hand, I attempted to explain how I was feeling judged and condemned by them. They did not agree that it was wrong to constantly point out my obvious (to them) shortcomings to others. It was their opinion of me, against my own opinion of me. There was nothing I could say to help them understand how much this hurt me and made them look prideful to others. When we tried to bring in other leaders to mediate the situation it became one big game of "they said," "we said."

In my heart, I persistently asked God to help me know how to deal with this situation. I wanted to be sincerely humble, but I felt like I could never do that while I tried to defend myself. This was an intense season of prayer and fasting for my husband and me. One night God woke me up with a specific chapter of the Bible in mind, and I woke my husband up and told him. He went to our roof, alone. Hours went by as he read and prayed. God lead him very specifically to the decision that we should remove ourselves from the harmful situation.

After a hurtful split between our family and this leadership, I asked God to help me understand how to handle the backlash. God told me to stop my defense of our reputation. I felt God lead me to the story of Saul and David in the book of 1 Samuel. Saul disobeys God, and as a direct result loses the kingship that he feels defines him as a person. God has the prophet anoint David as the new king. At the same time, Saul becomes increasingly hostile toward David because of David's success on the battlefield. Eventually, the situation turns into a huge game of cat and mouse where Saul chases David and continually attempts to murder him. As the chase continues, David refuses to utilize the many opportunities he has to kill Saul. David tells his military advisers that Saul is God's anointed, and God will deal with it in God's timing.

I do not mean to imply that the other people in my situation were acting like Saul, only that God used this example to encourage me to behave as David did. As our previous leadership made a very public announcement about our betrayal, we remained positive, asserting our love and support for them in their calling. Through this ordeal, I was able to learn an important lesson about sincere humility.

One of the biggest mistakes that I made during that time in my life was to accept the criticisms against me, without testing them according to the light of God's word. It is true that to have humility means that we should be able to receive correction; this is an important part of spiritual growth. It is also true that we must be teachable. When we receive correction that lines up with what the Bible says, we should be able to repent and learn from these warnings. However, we have to be careful to test whatever correction we receive against the Word of God. There will be people in all of our lives who are difficult to please. Unfortunately, some of these people will be Christians.

Just because someone is a Christian does not mean that their opinions are more important than what the Bible says. We know that, as members of God's creation, each of our individual personalities is uniquely created. If someone does not like a non-sinful aspect of my personality, it is their responsibility to die to themselves (get over their personal preferences), not demand that I change the person God has created me to be. The reverse is also true. If I am annoyed by a particular personality trait in someone else and it is not sinful, I must pray and ask God to change my heart toward this characteristic, in humility and submission to God's will for that person. It would be wrong and sinful for me to impose my personal preferences on someone else.

Don't Exchange the Truth for a Lie

God's opinion must be the ultimate standard, and the best way to find out His opinion is to study His Word. Real repentance is a fruit of true humility. If we spend time with God, reading His Word and asking Him to teach us to be sincerely humble, He will help us recognize when we are truly being warned by brothers and sisters about a sinful behavior or attitude we possess. He will also help us discern if someone else is imposing their will and preference on us, while they wrongfully insist we are in sin. It is never wise to exchange truth for a lie.

My True Defense

Another important aspect of humility is to resist the temptation to defend yourself against other people. Matthew 5:38-39 says, *"You have heard that it was said, 'An eye for an eye and a tooth for a tooth.' But I tell you not to resist an evil person. But whoever slaps you on your right*

41

cheek, turn the other to him also." Jesus did not mean this in reference to a violent attack. He used the illustration of being slapped on the cheek because this is a personal offense, such as an attack against a person's character or them being called a name. Jesus is using an Old Testament illustration, "an eye for an eye," to show us that, according to His updated teachings, we should not try to exact vengeance when someone hurts our feelings. However, this does not mean we have to accept what is said to be true if it is not. There is a difference between humility, which places others above me, and the acceptance of pride as wisdom. Apparently, that was a lesson I needed to learn the hard way. True humility does not mean that I look for opportunities to feel bad about my life and enter into self-pity. True humility seeks after God. It yearns for blamelessness and true repentance of sin, understanding that until that happens, God's grace has me covered.

PERFECT HUMILITY

"And being found in appearance as a man, He humbled Himself and became obedient to the point of death, even the death of the cross." –Philippians 2:8

Here we see that Jesus, also known as God's Son in human form, humbled Himself to the point of dying on the cross. He was putting others above Himself. He took on a punishment He did not deserve. If we look back at Jesus' entire ministry throughout the four gospels, we never see Him exercise His power over anyone in a forceful way. He always gives people the option to choose whether they want to follow Him. He could demand to be worshipped, and rightfully so, but He doesn't.

Jesus put everyone that has ever lived on this planet

(or will ever live in the future) above Himself when He took the punishment for the sins of the world and died on the cross. Jesus Christ is the purest example we have of sincere humility.

Let me end this chapter with a comparison that I hope will help you embrace humility and reject pride. Humility is the quiet confidence in God that allows you to receive correction, in the knowledge that God still loves you and wants to make you into a blameless and righteous creation. Humility boldly asserts that God's word is right, in a loving and encouraging way that does not aim to make me personally right at the expense of another. Pride is the loud person in the room, saying how right they are, willing to sacrifice everyone else's feelings. Pride wants to destroy the quiet confidence in God that humility longs to embrace, and replace it with confidence in ourselves. Which one do you want directing your life? The one that leads to destruction, or the one that leads to honor and a deeper relationship with Jesus? Do you want to be like Jesus, or like Satan? I would rather be like Jesus. After all, Jesus cared enough about me to sacrifice Himself. What good thing did Satan, or pride, ever do for me? Not one thing.

"But if you have bitter envy and self-seeking in your hearts, do not boast and lie against the truth. This wisdom does not descend from above, but is earthly, sensual, demonic. For where envy and self-seeking exist, confusion and every evil thing are there. But the wisdom that is from above is first pure, then peaceable, gentle, willing to yield, full of mercy and good fruits, without partiality and without hypocrisy. Now the fruit of righteousness is sown in peace by those who make peace." -James 3:14-18

CHAPTER 5

CONFIDENCE CONCEPTS THAT ARE NOT FOUND IN THE BIBLE

You may wonder why I would even want to talk about these terms that are not in the Bible. I agree that the Bible has all of the answers that we need in order to understand our worthiness of love (and everything else we need to know). However, the Bible also warns us to be wise about the philosophical ideas that are popular in the world. In recent times, we have seen the increase of supposed Bible teachers, embracing these unbiblical concepts and teaching them to Christians as if they actually did come from the Bible. Some teachers push certain ideas on the flock of Jesus Christ that Jesus never wanted us to be concerned with. Look at Colossians 2:8, *"Beware lest anyone cheat you through philosophy and empty deceit, according to the tradition of men, according to the basic principles of the world, and not according to Christ."* We also see that to write books and teach about concepts like self-hatred, self-esteem, and personal insecurity is extremely profitable.

In many books on this topic, the authors communicate that they believe the reason insecurity is such a problem in our present society is due to the fact that many people feel bad about who they are and this sucks all the joy from their lives. Insecurity and lack of joy are blamed for causing difficulties in people's relationships. I disagree with this assessment. I do not believe that the cause of these major problems in relationships has to do with a lack of personal joy or with being insecure. My belief is that many difficulties in relationships are consequences of the unrepentant sin of pride.

Join me in my quest to use God's word as a flashlight to illuminate the truth—that insecurity (low self-esteem) and lack of personal joy are not to blame for feelings of personal worthlessness or dysfunction in our relationships. As someone who previously accepted these lies, I understand how destructive they are.

CONCEPT #1: SELF-HATRED

Get ready to stretch your brain. We're going to talk about different terminology in the realm of self-appraisal. But don't worry, I promise to break everything down so that these ideas are easy to understand. The reason I want to spend a significant time on this topic is because the term "self-hatred" seems to appear frequently in Christian books and Bible studies that aim to help you become a more confident person. I have read sentences like the following many times:

"God doesn't want you to suffer from self-hatred. He wants you to have victory, and until you love yourself, He can't deliver you from your lack of personal confidence."

This kind of thinking (and writing) worries me because in my research, I have not found one character example of self-hatred in the Bible. I think we should take a minute to define this mysterious concept before we talk about it in more detail. We know what "self" means. It has to do with your own person, yourself. It is the term we use when we speak about ourselves. My self is me, and your self is you. Now let's look at the term "hatred." According to the dictionary, hate can be defined as a very strong aversion [3]. Based on both of these individual definitions we can determine that self-hatred means that a person has an extreme dislike for themselves.

As a person who was caught up in what the world calls self-hatred, I feel qualified to give you an inside look into the mind of a person that struggles with it. When I would say things like, "I hate myself," what I really meant was, "I wish other people liked me more." When I had thoughts like, "I'm worthless, I might as well commit suicide," what I really meant was, "I feel like no one else values me, I might as well not exist." Looking to the definition we came up with for self-hatred, I did not actually hate myself. I wanted to be valued by others more. I wanted to feel worthy of love. I did not hate myself, because if I actually disliked myself, I would not want others to like me. If I truly disliked myself, I would want other people to hate me as well. According to what I have found in the Bible and my own personal experience with self-hatred, I am going to advocate for the opinion that "self-hatred" does not actually exist. Subsequently, in God's word we find this little gem:

"For no one ever hated his own flesh, but nourishes and cherishes it, just as the Lord does the church," -Ephesians 5:29.

In context, this verse is talking about marriage and how a husband should love their wife "as their own bodies." However, this verse also makes a very significant statement in further explanation of what it means when a husband loves their own body. The Bible says that no one ever hates their own flesh. According to Ephesians 5:29, self-hatred doesn't exist.

We can also discredit the term "self-hatred" based on human logic. Because the Bible says it doesn't exist is enough of an argument for me, but for those who feel I might be taking Ephesians 5:29 out of context, let's go further. Just because one throws two words together that are valid and mean something individually, does not mean that together they create an actual, plausible concept or idea. According to the definition of self-hatred, one feels unloved or worthless because one dislikes who one is. But when we use self-hatred, what we really mean is that we desire to feel loved and worthy. Wanting to feel loved and worthy are both positive concepts. If we truly hated ourselves, we would not desire for positive things to happen to us. When we struggle with anger and hatred toward someone else, we don't say, "I hope that person gets a thousand blessings!" We desire the opposite for them, we wish for them to have negative experiences. We might think something like, "I hope they get what they deserve," and the connotation of that "thing they deserve" is always bad.

Self-hatred is not in our nature, but self-love is. If we attempt to think logically we might say, well if self-love is pride, then isn't the opposite of pride equal to self-hate? The short answer is no. Many Christians actively argue that since the opposite of pride is humility, the opposite of self-love must be self-hatred. In order for this to be true, it would mean that humility is the same thing as self-hatred. It is not. Self-hatred refuses to acknowledge that as a created being of God we are worthy of His love, which is unbiblical. Humility means that one puts others above their own interests because one understands their own littleness when compared to God. The motivation for this selflessness is not because you hate yourself, but because you love God and others more than you love yourself. Did Jesus hate Himself? No. Previously we saw Jesus as the ultimate example of humility. If you subscribe to the belief that the opposite of pride must be self-hatred, you are also subscribing to the idea that Jesus died on the cross because He hated Himself. Jesus actually died on the cross because of His intense love for us, not for any other reason. *"But God, who is rich in mercy, because of His great love with which He loved us, even when we were dead in trespasses, made us alive together with Christ—by grace you have been saved."* - Ephesians 2:5

Self-hatred is not real; it does not actually exist, nor is it equivalent to humility.

CONCEPT #2: SELF-ESTEEM

When I prepared to write the first edition of this book, God had just shown me that my low self-esteem was actually a type of sinful pride, and I wanted to find out more about the concept of self-esteem. I used an internet Bible search engine to look up every verse in the Bible that contains the word "self." It intrigued me that none of those verses talked about creating your own self worth. Then I looked up "esteem" as well, yet I could not find anything positive in regards to esteeming one's own self. Don't take my word for it, go research it on your own. I am confident that you will come to the same conclusion I did. Once I realized that self-esteem was not a biblical concept, I wanted to find out where it came from.

After hours of research and looking through dozens of .edu websites, I found the first mentions of self-esteem. In the United States, its first appearance was as a psychological concept in a book by Dr. Morris Rosenberg, a professor in the Department of Sociology in the College of Behavioral and Social Sciences at the University of Maryland. His widely cited book is titled, *Society and the Adolescent Image* [4]. This book was published in 1965, and in it we see the first use of self-esteem as a tool for evaluating a person's psychology. Though it was Rosenberg who created a specific method to evaluate self-esteem, the term didn't become well-known until another doctor popularized the concept. In his book *The Power of Self-Esteem*, written in 1987, Dr. Nathaniel Branden popularized the self-esteem movement in psychology. According to his most updated definition, not everything he lists is necessarily problematic, but there are two parts of the definition I want to discuss in light of what the Bible teaches. Due to copyright laws, I have paraphrased the first two (and most important) parts of Dr. Branden's definition of self-esteem.

Self-esteem is:

1. When I deem that I myself am able to consider and deal with the difficulties in this life alone. [5]

2. When I decide I have ability to emphasize my rights to happiness, my rights to feelings of worthiness, to

demand my needs and wants from others, and to enjoy the fruitful results of all my personal efforts. [5]

Please read the two parts again and think about the biblical lens we developed in the previous chapter. If we look at these two parts of Dr Branden's definition and think back to the definition of pride, there are striking similarities. In fact, I think we should look at the definition of pride again. Pride is "the quality or state of being proud; inordinate self-esteem; an unreasonable conceit of one's own superiority in talents, beauty, wealth, rank, etc., which manifests itself in lofty airs, distance, reserve, and often in contempt of others" [1]. Asserting our rights, needs, and wants fits neatly under the feelings that we have superiority and deserve respect. See what I did there?

Having confidence in my own ability to deal with the challenges of life leaves no room to depend on God. In Proverbs 3:5-6 we see that God instructs us to do the exact opposite of what Dr. Branden suggests: "Trust in the Lord with all your heart, and lean not on your own understanding; in all your ways acknowledge Him, and He shall direct your paths."

In the second half of Dr. Branden's definition, we see that having self-esteem also means that we should emphasize our rights to happiness and feelings of worthiness, and that we must demand our needs and wants from others. Now, think back to our discussion about humility. If one understands their "moral littleness," and is submissive to others, will they emphasize their needs and wants? Did Jesus want to die on the cross? According to Matthew 28:39, where we are able to tune into the prayers of Jesus right before He is taken into custody, He did not. "He went a little farther and fell on His face, and prayed, saying, 'O My Father, if it is possible, let this cup pass from Me; nevertheless, not as I will, but as You will." Jesus asked if He could avoid dying on the cross, but ultimately submitted to God the Father's will.

There is another section of this definition that you might be tempted to overlook. This is especially true since Christian self-help books, found in Christian households throughout the world, espouse this popular, yet unbiblical, idea. In the second half of the definition of self-esteem, Dr. Branden states that to have self-esteem means that we must emphasize our right to happiness. This implies that within ourselves, we should be able to produce our own happiness. There is now a powerful movement lead by another well-known doctor, Kristin Neff, that emphasizes the same idea under the term self-compassion. If you listen to Dr. Neff's most popular TEDx Talk (where she argues against the value of self-esteem), you will hear her say that if you just give yourself some compassion when you make mistakes or are having a hard time, you will have a better life. I'm not saying we shouldn't have compassion for ourselves. God extends grace and mercy to us, and we should remember to extend those same things to ourselves when we feel like failures. My problem with her argument is that ultimately it is the same as that of Dr. Branden's in that they both believe you can create your own happiness. The difference is that Dr. Branden believes you can achieve this by utilizing self-esteem while Dr. Neff believes you must utilize self-compassion. This trend isn't anything new and I'm sure it's not going to go away anytime soon.

<u>Can You Create Your Own Happiness?</u>

I cannot find anything in the Bible that tells us we are able to create our own happiness. In Proverbs 3:13 we see, "Happy is the man who finds wisdom, and the man who gains understanding." So if we find wisdom and understanding we will be happy? Well yes, that is the idea, however we need to think about the context of this verse. What kind of wisdom and understanding? The kind we can learn from books? The kind we get from listening to TEDx talks? No, that is not the type of wisdom or understanding this verse discusses. If you continue to read through Proverbs 3, you will see it specifically talks about the wisdom and understanding that comes directly from God.

"The Lord by wisdom founded the earth; by understanding He established the heavens." -Proverbs 3:19

This is the godly wisdom and knowledge we need, and only by it will we find happiness. Maybe you think that I am being too literal, and I need to look beyond the word "happy." Perhaps I need a synonym. Okay, let's take a look at "joy" in the Bible. Surely there is something in there about being able to create my own joy. There are 150 verses in the New King James Version of the Bible that contain the word joy. In contrast, there is not one verse where joy is the result of self-searching. Joy is always the result of God's presence, God's blessings, God's justice, or the fellowship found with other believers.

"You will show me the path of life; in Your presence is fullness of joy; At your right hand are pleasures forevermore." -Psalm 16:11

Works of the Flesh vs. Works of the Spirit

In order to take this comparison one step further, we need to look into the works of the flesh and the fruits of the spirit. According to the definition of self-esteem we should have the ability to create our own happiness, worthiness, and the positive things we deserve. However, in the Bible we see two distinct categories of ability. Works of the flesh are things that we are able to do in our own power; we have the ability to create them within ourselves. Fruits of the Spirit, however, have to come from God's Spirit. We are unable to create them on our own in our flesh. Let's take a look at which abilities fit into each group.

"Now the works of the flesh are evident, which are: adultery, fornication, uncleanness, lewdness, idolatry, sorcery, hatred, contentions, jealousies, outbursts of wrath, selfish ambitions, dissensions, heresies, envy, murders, drunkenness, revelries, and the like; of which I tell you beforehand, just as I also told you in time past, that those who practice such things will not inherit the kingdom of God. But the fruit of the Spirit is love, joy, peace, longsuffering, kindness, goodness, faithfulness, gentleness, self-control. Against such there is no law. And those who are Christ's have crucified the flesh with its passions and desires." -Galatians 5:19-24

There you have it. Joy is not a fruit of the flesh. However, selfish ambitions, contentions, and envy are, and that means according to the Bible that these are sinful. If you want to fully agree with the definition and concept of self-esteem, you have to disagree with God's word. That means you must directly disagree with God.

The reason I wanted to talk so much about self-esteem is because I want to point out that it is not a biblical concept. Self-esteem is a principle that many preachers and Christian authors emphasize, but it is, in fact, a worldly concept that contradicts the teaching of the Bible. Esteeming one's self is a form of pride, and it is considered a sin. We cannot keep advocating for better self-esteem in believers and end up with people that have been delivered from the sinful burden of pride. The only way to be delivered from sin is to confess and repent. By continuing to push the concept of self-esteem on believers, we will continually handicap their spiritual growth through the encouragement of a sinful behavior. I am not saying that every person is unworthy of love or esteem, but I am saying that one's value cannot be found in one's self. In the next chapter, I will explain God's plan regarding godly confidence for each individual believer.

However, before we can do that, there is one last non-biblical concept we need to cover.

CONCEPT #3: IGNORING OUR INSECURITIES

How many times have you heard someone tell you or another person that it's best just not to think about their feelings? "Oh, you don't like that? Just don't think about it," people will advise. But ignoring our insecurities instead of dealing with them is a temptation from Satan that gets many of us into trouble. For that reason, I want to devote extra time to understanding why ignoring our individual doubts is unwise.

There are areas in all of our lives that make us feel insecure. Even the most prideful people have insecurities, and often they use their pride in an attempt to mask their true feelings. In order to help you understand what your personal uncertainties may be, we are going to break down all insecurities into three categories. These three groups are physical appearance and ability, intellectual ability, and spiritual ability. Now let's take a look at examples that fit into each group.

Storytime

Mary is at the beach and a few friends are getting ready to play beach volleyball. Mary refuses to play, and offers the explanation that she isn't any good at sports. Mary's friends assure her that it's just a game for fun and they would love for her to join, but Mary refuses. She watches closely, secretly wishing she could play and laugh with them, but she knows she would never let herself risk a potentially embarrassing moment. Have you ever felt like Mary? I know I have. In this scenario, Mary is insecure about her physical ability to play a sport. She does not have any physical limitations in her body itself, like an injury or disability. Even though the game is just for fun, her insecurity in this area is keeping her from enjoying this aspect of life. If nothing changes in Mary, she will continually make the choice to miss fun opportunities she actually wants to participate in.

Time to meet John. He is a really fun guy that everyone loves to be around. John's friends invite him to go swimming at the pool, but John declines. He says he is not a good swimmer. John makes everything the group does more enjoyable, so his friends continue to prompt him. He finally agrees to go down to the pool, but wears jeans and a t-shirt to make it known that he has no plans to go in the water. The truth is, John is a wonderful swimmer, but he is insecure about how he looks with his shirt off. He knows that to swim with his shirt on will only draw more attention to this insecurity, so he refuses the swim altogether. Until something changes in John, he will attempt to be satisfied with solo swims. The insecurities that plague both Mary and John fall under the category of physical ability and appearance.

Allow me to introduce you to Elizabeth. She works at a very popular bank. She has been there for five years, and despite the fact that she is a hard worker, she feels like her boss notices only her colleagues. One of the workers with a private office and desk has plans to move to a different branch soon, and Elizabeth wants to make sure that she is the one that gets promoted into that position. She daydreams about the things she will hang on the wall, and how she will be able to boss her former colleagues around. While everyone else gets their bags and jackets, she spends the last few minutes of her day in a mad dash to rearrange her workmate's files. She knows this workmate will be reprimanded the next day, but no serious harm will come to them. And as a result of these events, she will stand out as an obvious choice and most competent person to receive the promotion. Elizabeth feels like once she gets the promotion, she will finally be able to prove to her prideful father that he has been wrong about her. She wants to show him that she is not the huge disappointment he says she is. Once she proves her worth to him, maybe she will finally be able to forget all the nasty names he called her during her childhood. Elizabeth's insecurities are intellectual. Since she spent her childhood being told how stupid she was by her father, she does not believe she will be considered valuable by anyone until she can prove her intellectual abilities are superior to theirs. Caught up in her destructive cycle, she will eventually commit a more serious deception, get caught, and lose her job.

Grace is a dedicated member of the church. She shows up early every Sunday morning to prepare for the 2nd grade class she teaches each week. Yet, outside of her Sunday School class, she does not have many friends. She sits by herself at Sunday night service, and only a few people in the Children's ministry know her name. Grace keeps quiet and avoids people who may try to include her in group events. She is afraid that if the people at church get to know her better, they will reject her and she will feel even lonelier. Every night before she goes to sleep, she prays for God to change her personality and help her forget the sarcastic comments of the mean girls from her high school. She doesn't trust that God created her with a specific personality, or that He wants to use her in a bigger way. Grace is overcome by a spiritual insecurity that has her trapped in self-imposed isolation. She is terrified by what rejections may happen if she completely places her trust in God.

Can You Relate?

Perhaps you relate to one of the three types of insecurities. If you are anything like me, you may identify with all three. Insecurities come from different places and experiences; they might stem from a difficult family relationship, originate due to peer behavior, or form on their own in our sinful hearts as we choose to believe the lies of Satan over the truths of God. But, we are created beings, handcrafted by our Heavenly Father. It is never God's will for us to question His creation.

As a son or daughter of the King, you are God's creation. He made you a specific way for a definitive purpose. It is true that He longs to help us grow in righteousness and put off the sinful man (Colossians 3:9-10), but that is a separate issue from the one we have discussed here. Insecurities happen when we question God's creation. Satan hopes to make us feel worthless with his ability to target specific uncertainty in each of us. Conviction is the feeling we get from the Holy Spirit when we sin, in order to turn us to repentance. This is a significant distinction.

Satan wants you to believe that God made a mistake when God created you. On the other hand, God wants you to know He loves you, and desires to deliver you from the bondage of sin. We need to get to the point where, as the body of Christ, we are able to understand these are two different experiences. In confession, repentance, and humility, God has given us the tools to battle against sin. But remember, humility is defined as understanding our moral littleness compared to God, not in the belief that as individuals we are worthless. So how does God teach us to deal with the insecurities Satan continually throws in our faces?

Before we get to the answer of that question, we need to look at the way that the church deals with insecurity in general. I pray that there are churches out there that are helping people gain victory over their personal insecurities on an individual level. Unfortunately, most fellowships that I have been part of do not do this. It seems to me that the way Christians deal with personal uncertainties is to ignore these doubts altogether. We hope that if we do so, our insecurities will go away, and in the meantime, we avoid doing things that will expose them. For many years, I went along with this train of thought. I avoided conversations about my personal doubts and any kind of activity that had the potential to expose my true feelings or make me uncomfortable. I also never encouraged anyone else to share their insecurities with me. Being a part of a quiet crowd gave me anonymity. After my journey into what God's word says about confidence issues, I realized that I have never seen the concept of ignoring one's insecurities as a positive way for dealing with them in the Bible. I have not read instructions from God that His children should hold their personal uncertainties close and let them inhibit spiritual growth. I believe that there are churches and books out there that encourage the church body to deal with insecurities in a biblical way, but in my experience, they are not the norm. As a church we need to confront our individual doubts, talk about them, and look at how God deals with these topics in the Bible. Let's look at two examples.

GOOD OLD MO

When I think of the word, "insecurity," there are two Bible characters that immediately come to mind. Let's start with the most obvious. Which Old Testament leader repeatedly questions God when it comes to God's choice of him as a leader? Moses rejects God's primary plan for him on the basis of his own insecurities more than once. If you read Exodus chapters 3 and 4, you will see what I mean, but let's go through a quick overview of what happened. God appears to Moses in a burning bush—a bush on fire, but not actually consumed. After God introduces Himself, Moses realizes it is the Almighty God talking to him, and God tells Moses that He sees how the people of Israel suffer. God has a plan to deliver His people, and Moses has been chosen to lead the campaign. Even though we can tell Moses recognizes God—which is evident by the fear Moses displays—the first thing Moses does when he hears this awesome plan is to question God. In Exodus 3:11 we read Moses' plea, *"But Moses said to God, 'Who am I that I should go to Pharaoh, and that I should bring the children out of Egypt?'"* But God is patient with Moses. He tells Moses how to respond in the situation that Moses is afraid to face.

Moses is not focused on God's mighty hand, or God's ability to overcome any situation—He looks instead at his own limitations. He lets his personal insecurities dictate his response to God's call on his life. But God reminds Moses that He will be with him. As the conversation continues, God gives Moses very specific instructions about everything that will happen. Moses is quiet and listens until God finishes the explanation of His plan. For a moment there is a glimmer of hope that Moses understands that God will help him complete this mission. But then Moses starts to speak...

Then Moses answered and said, "But suppose they will not believe me or listen to my voice; suppose they say, 'The Lord has not appeared to you.'" So the Lord said to him, "What is that in your hand?" He said, "A rod." And He said, "Cast it on the ground." So he cast it on the ground, and it became a serpent; and Moses fled from it. Then the Lord said to Moses, "Reach out your hand and take it by the tail" (and he reached out his hand and caught it, and it became a rod in his hand), "that they may believe that the Lord God of their fathers, the God of Abraham, the God of Isaac, and the God of Jacob, has appeared to you. -Exodus 4:1-5

It may appear that Moses doubts the ability of the people to understand God's plan, but God's answer to this problem does not convince Moses. God gives Moses three distinct signs that the people will be able to recognize: the rod that turns into a snake, the ability to turn his hand leprous and heal it, and the ability to make water into blood on dry land (Exodus 4:4-9). Moses is still not persuaded that this is a good plan, and finally divulges his specific fear to God.

Then Moses said to the Lord, "Oh my Lord, I am not eloquent neither before nor since you have spoken to Your servant; but I am slow of speech and slow of tongue. So the Lord said to him, "Who has made man's mouth? Or who makes the mute, the deaf, the seeing, or the blind? Have not I, the Lord? Now therefore, go, and I will be with your mouth and teach you what you shall say." But he said, "O my Lord, please send by the hand of whomever else You may send." So the anger of the Lord was kindled against Moses, and He said, "Is not Aaron the Levite your brother? I know that he can speak well. And look, he is also coming out to meet you. When he sees you, he will be glad in his heart. Now you shall speak to him and put the words in his mouth. And I will be with your mouth and with his mouth, and I will teach you what you shall do. So he shall be your spokesman to the people. And he himself shall be as a mouth for you, and you shall be to him as God. -Exodus 4:10-16

Moses is insecure about his ability to speak eloquently—he is apprehensive about his intellectual ability. In Exodus 4:11, God responds to this specific insecurity that Moses has with a reminder that God has made the blind and the mute. God attempts to help Moses focus on the truth, that God is the one who created Moses' mouth and intellectual ability to speak. God has more than equipped Moses to perform the tasks that God is asking him to execute. God also reassures Moses that He will be with him, and teach him what to say.

God shares the truth with Moses, but Moses does not want to hear it. He replies to God, "Lord, can You send someone else? I can't to do this." This is a blatant rejection of God's will. God has shown Moses that as His creation, God has given Moses the ability to do what He asks him to do, but He doesn't force Moses to obey. At this point we get a glimpse into God's frustration in verse 14: *"So the anger of the Lord was kindled against Moses..."* But in His loving grace and mercy, God offers Moses an alternative option. God sets up a supernatural game of telephone.

God tells Moses what to say, Moses then tells his brother Aaron, and Aaron is the spokesperson for the cause. If this seems needlessly complicated to you, good, you get the point. It is not God's plan to play this supernatural game of telephone, but because of Moses' insecurities, God gives him an alternate route. God's amazing plan is thwarted, and after Moses' refusal to abide by this procedure, God could choose not to use him. But instead, God shows grace and mercy to Moses. Because of this, God has to alter His already perfect system. This plan change is the consequence of Moses' refusal to choose victory in God over his personal insecurities. What a bummer.

There are several important lessons we can learn from this chunk of scripture. The first thing we can glean from this incident is that God has not created us to have insecurities. He doesn't tell Moses to be fearful in this area. He wants to deliver Moses from his insecurity by reminding him that He, the All-Powerful Creator of the universe, is the one that made Moses. The same thing applies to us. God created us, and He is able to help us complete any task that He asks us to do. God shows His care for Moses in the way he takes time to extract the underlying issue. According to 1 Samuel 16:7, God can see directly into all of our hearts. Despite His awareness, God lovingly attempts to work through a particular problem that His son Moses has. God desires to do the same things in our lives. He wants us to confess our insecurities to Him so that He can remind us that He has made us and He will help us. One way we can approach this in the body of Christ is to acknowledge our insecurities to one another, and remind each other that God is the One that created us. God does not make any mistakes, and in His creative plan for us as His children, He is purposeful and specific. In the end, we see that God will not force us to overcome our insecurities. I cannot help but wonder what would have happened if Moses obeyed God and acted as the Lord's mouthpiece.

THE FLEECER, GIDEON

Now let's take a look at a Bible character that fits into a different insecurity group. I'm sure you've met him before, but let me remind you. Allow me to introduce my doubtful friend Gideon. I wish I wasn't so much like him, but at times I am. For his story we need to fast forward past Moses. At this point, the Israelites have already been delivered from Egypt. They enter into the Promised Land, quickly forget that God is the one who delivered them, and proceed to worship other gods. Consequently, they are taken captive and have everything taken from them by the Midianites, as a form of judgement for their treatment of God. In our first glimpse of Gideon, Judges chapter 6, he has been out by the winepress threshing wheat in secret so that the Midianites will not take his family's food. Israel has started to feel sorry for seeking after other gods, and begins to cry out to the true God again. In response, God sends the Angel of the Lord (aka Jesus, pre-human body) to Gideon in Judges 6:12, *"And the Angel of the Lord appeared to him, and said to him, 'The Lord is with you, you mighty man of valor!'"* God has chosen Gideon to save Israel from the hand of the Midianites, and He sends the Angel of the Lord to deliver the news. Pay attention to what happens next in verse 15, *"So he said to Him, 'O my Lord, how can I save Israel? Indeed my clan is the weakest in Manasseh, and I am the least in my father's house."* As we read through the story, we start to recognize the familiar pattern of personal insecurity. I think we should take a minute at this point to look at two seemingly contradicting statements in this text.

We need to contrast what the Lord says with Gideon's response. We are about to witness a meeting between Gideon and the Angel of the Lord. But first we need a quick moment aside to discuss who the Angel of the Lord is. Let's go straight to the scripture.

Now the Angel of the Lord came and sat under the terebinth tree which was Ophrah, which belonged to Joash the Abiezrite, while his son Gideon threshed wheat in the winepress, in order to hide it from the Midianites. And the Angel of the Lord appeared to him, and said to him, "The Lord is with you, you mighty man of valor!" Gideon said to Him, "O my Lord, if the Lord is with us, why then has all this happened to us? And where are all His miracles which our fathers told us about saying, 'Did not the Lord bring us up from Egypt?' But now the Lord has forsaken us and delivered us into the hands of the Midianites." Then the Lord turned to him and said, "Go in this might of yours, and you shall save Israel from the hand of the Midianites. Have I not sent you?" So he said to Him, "O my Lord, how can I save Israel? Indeed my clan is the weakest in Manasseh, and I am the least in my father's house. -Judges 6:11-15

If you pay close attention to the passage we just read, you will notice that Gideon switches from talking to "the Angel of the Lord" to the "Lord." This is because the Angel of the Lord is actually a Christophany. A Christophany is an appearance of Christ, before He comes to Earth in a human body as Jesus. Remember that Gideon is actually having a conversation with Christ, who existed before the foundations of the world (John 1:1). When the Angel of the Lord first addresses Gideon, He calls him a mighty man of valor. Gideon is the man. This is the Old Testament, people! Can you imagine how cool it would have been to have the Angel of the Lord visit you and call you mighty? I would have been elated. But Gideon doesn't seem excited. In fact, he questions God's selection in his mention that his family history is the worst in reputation. The Lord says that Gideon is a mighty man of valor, but Gideon contends that he is not. Who is telling the truth?

Since God cannot lie (Titus 1:2) and He sent the Angel of the Lord, the Angel must be the one telling the truth. Gideon has a perverted view of the situation, and as a result he questions God's plan. This is what spiritual insecurities do to people. Remember that in the beginning of Judges 6, we got a glimpse into the fearful character of Gideon. We initially find him hiding from the enemy where he threshes wheat in the winepress. Further on in the chapter, we read that God gives Gideon an inside look—He reveals His specific, creative purposes for Gideon's life. God has the Angel of the Lord tell Gideon what Gideon actually is—a mighty man of valor—but Gideon doesn't believe the Angel. Once again, it goes back to that same, tired line that Satan has repeatedly fed us, "Did God really say...?"

You might be thinking that the reason Gideon gives for not being the one to save Israel is weak. You are correct. The "weak family history," excuse has got to be one of the lamest excuses ever seen in the Bible. Let's go back to the text for the Angel's response. *"And the Lord said to him, 'Surely I will be with you, and you shall defeat the Midianites as one man."* Here in verse 16 we see that God has planned to take down the entire Midianite army through one man, Gideon. But Gideon isn't convinced. At this point, Gideon starts to test God to see if He is who He says He is. Gideon's actions come from a standpoint of terror instead of victory, despite God's assurances. Does God still use Gideon? Yes, incredibly, God continues to use him. It is apparent though that Gideon doesn't trust God the way he should. Gideon is spiritually insecure in God's ability to do what God says He will do.

Because of Gideon we have the popular phrase, "fleecing God." Judges 6:37 reads, *"So Gideon said to God, 'If You will save Israel by my hand as You have said – look, I shall put a fleece of wool on the threshing floor; if there is dew on the fleece only, and it is dry on all the ground, then I shall know that You will save Israel by my hand, as You have said."*

Then Gideon proceeds to test God again, with the opposite test, a dry fleece and wet ground. If you are going to "fleece God," you should keep in mind that it is a symptom of spiritual insecurity. Either you choose to trust God, or you choose to doubt Him. You can't have it both ways. If you want to read the rest of Gideon's story to find out how it all pans out, you can find it in Judges chapters 6 through 8. In my opinion, the end is pretty depressing for a mighty man of valor.

Gideon, Me, and Myself

There are several important lessons we can learn from Gideon. He is the spokesperson of spiritual insecurity. For the purpose of clarity, I will define spiritual insecurity as any insecurity that causes one to question God. You may remember that when I first introduced you to Gideon, I made a remark about how alike he and I are. You see, the main insecurity Gideon has is in God. He doesn't trust God to do what God says He will do. I have been guilty of that same insecurity. It took me ten years to learn that it was worthwhile to trust God. If ten years seems like a really long time to learn this lesson, it was. It took so long because I refused to trust God over and over. Even when God showed me through each new trial that I could trust Him, I refused. He remained faithful, but I was messing up His plan, just like Gideon.

I kept hearing that annoying voice that I thought was self-doubt say things like, "Does God really mean it when He says He has plans for you full of hope? Is God genuine when He says that He loves you? Is God sincere when He says that He will provide for you? Surely God cannot do all of these things, can He?" Lies, lies, lies! Satan is such a liar. God will do all of those things, and more. What I needed was a smack to the face with the truth of God's word. I'm sure Gideon would have benefited from something similar had he been willing to receive it.

Now, when I look back, all I can say is, "Shame on you, Kristin. Shame on you for being insecure in God's ability to love and take care of you. You ignored your insecurities for ten years, when God could have brought you so much peace, joy, and spiritual growth." Thankfully God's grace and mercy cover all of my mistakes. Like Hebrews 4:6 says, *"Let us therefore come boldly to the throne of grace, that we may obtain mercy and find grace to help in time of need."*

I beg you, fellow believers, let's have conversations about our uncertainties and insecurities. Find a mature, loving Christian that can listen to all of your concerns, and help dispel each one by going through verses that apply to each issue. Make sure you use wisdom and look for someone that is bearing spiritual fruit (Galatians 5), so you can avoid unnecessary and hurtful gossip. We must purpose in our hearts to stop doubting God, and instead to choose to believe everything He says.

If we continue to ignore our insecurities, we will never arrive at the victorious place that God desires for us. We are His children whom He loves so dearly, and He made us to be free from the bondage and anxiety and doubt.

Perhaps you have been feeling convicted through these last two chapters. It could be that you realize you have been ignoring what the Bible says about pride and humility. It could also be that you have come to the realization that you have been relying on unbiblical concepts to achieve confidence in your life. There can be deliverance from each of these specific areas. The good news is that all we need to do to be set free from our sins is to repent. That means we need to be sorry for our sin, and actively attempt to stop doing it/them (turn away). God can change our habits if we will trust Him and allow Him to teach us the righteous and blameless way that He wants us to do things. Take some time, pray, and confess your sins to God right now. He has been waiting to hear from you. He wants to heal your heart.

"For no other foundation can anyone lay than that which is laid, which is Jesus Christ." -1 Corinthians 3:11

CHAPTER 6

THE LOVE THAT DEFINES US

As Christians, we are commanded by our Loving Father to give up sinful pride. But, if we follow that command, where can we find our worth? How will we determine our value, apart from feeling we deserve to be respected by others? These are valid and extremely important questions that we must answer if we are going to have sincere, godly confidence. These questions also drive us as individuals. In this chapter, I want to address the deepest insecurities that one can possess. I also want to answer the questions previously mentioned and share a sincere truth with you about how your Father in heaven sees you.

Earlier in the book, I mentioned that I was on a quest to feel loved. The compulsion to feel loved is one of the most basic needs that drives all human beings. My life has been defined by this need in such a way, that my favorite character in the entire Bible became a woman from John chapter 4. We don't know her name, but her story and longing are something that I identify with. Will you take a walk to ancient Samaria with me? I want to introduce you to someone I affectionately call, "Mrs. Thirsty." This story also gives us an intimate glimpse into the heart of Jesus—the most important person in my life.

Jesus came to Earth to die on the cross and save us from our sins. I am very grateful that He did. But there is something else Jesus did while He was on Earth that He considered to be an important mission. Jesus knew that people needed Him. He talked to all different kinds of people and ended up with various types of disciples and followers, including tax collectors and former prostitutes. Jesus didn't care about the cultural stigmas of the time—He was after individuals. As proof of this, we have the following account. Jesus was at a Samaritan well during the hottest part of the day, about to have a very interesting conversation with a Samaritan woman, whose heart had been broken for far too long.

Now Jacob's well was there. Jesus therefore, being wearied from His journey, sat thus by the well. It was about the sixth hour. A woman of Samaria came to draw water. Jesus said to her, "Give me a drink." For His disciples had gone away into the city to buy food. Then the woman of Samaria said to Him, "How is it that You, being a Jew, ask a drink from me, a Samaritan woman?" For Jews have no dealings with Samaritans. Jesus answered and said to her, "If you knew the gift of God, and who it is who says to you, 'Give Me a drink,' you would have asked Him, and He would have given you living water." The woman said to Him, "Sir, You have nothing to draw with, and the well is deep. Where then do You get that living water? Are you greater than our father Jacob, who gave us the well, and drank from it himself, as well as his sons and his livestock?" Jesus answered and said to her, "Whoever drinks of this water will thirst again, but whoever drinks of the water that I shall give him will never thirst. But the water that I shall give him will become in him a fountain of water springing up into everlasting life." The woman said to Him, "Sir, give me this water, that I may not thirst, nor come here to draw." Jesus said to her, "Go, call your husband, and come here." The woman answered and said, "I have no husband." Jesus said to her, "You have well said, 'I have no husband,' for you have had five husbands, and the one whom you now have is not your husband; in that you spoke truly." - John 4:6-18

Meet my friend, Mrs. Thirsty—the shameful adulteress who has been married five times unsuccessfully. This woman is going to the well in the middle of the day because no one else wants to be around her. She is an outcast. (Please keep that in mind: Jesus loves the outcasts just as much as He loves everyone else. Jesus went after those on the fringe of society during His ministry, including Mrs. Thirsty.) If you read the verse after this, you will find out that Mrs. Thirsty knows that the Messiah will come (4:25). She has searched for something to fulfill her, but it has not come to her naturally. She has been through five marriages and now she is living (and having sex) with a man she isn't married to. Back then, living with someone you were not married to was a big deal. It was considered a shameful behavior that would cause everyone to reject you openly. The worldly opinion of popular culture today tells us this kind of behavior is acceptable, but we know the Bible says it is not.

Mrs. Thirsty is desperate for something to give her life meaning. At first she thinks Jesus is talking about special water that will take away physical thirst, but at the end of this story we see that she understands Jesus. She leaves her water pot (4:28) to go tell everyone about her Lord and Savior.

Let me ask you a question. Do you think this woman, Mrs. Thirsty, the adulterer and outcast, left her water pot behind because she was no longer thirsty? She lived in the hot desert, okay? She was probably always thirsty, but she was no longer spiritually thirsty.

She has become spiritually fulfilled by Jesus Christ, the living water that causes her to thirst no more. In fact, she is excited that she has found the answer to the question of spiritual fulfillment, she runs to tell everyone in town. Remember that these are the same people that hate and despise her so much that she can't go to the well during the cool of the morning. Yet, she wants to tell them about Jesus. Her encounter with Jesus instantaneously gives her life meaning and takes away all of her shame—to the point where she becomes a bold evangelist for Jesus Christ!

There are so many lessons we could learn from this story, but let's focus on the issue of the desire to feel loved. I believe this account of Jesus and Mrs. Thirsty illustrates that we cannot be fulfilled by anything we can achieve in this world. Many women, like Mrs. Thirsty and me, have sought fulfillment in romantic relationships that can never compare to Jesus' pure, sincere, and powerful love.

A SINCERE & PERFECT LOVE

As I prayed about this chapter, I felt God's presences encourage me with the same thing over and over again, "Tell them I am IN love with them!" God wants you to know that those strong feelings that you feel (or desire to feel) for another living person are a smaller version of His intensely magnified love for you. For emphasis, let me repeat that a different way. God has created us in His image. Genesis 1:27 reads, *"So God created man in His own image; in the image of God He created him; male and female He created them."* One of the attributes God has given us that mirrors His own is the ability to feel emotions. God feels emotions in a way that we will never understand on this side of heaven. As a way to understand just a small taste of what God feels, He has given us our own set of human emotions. We feel joy, pain, anger, sadness, loneliness, regret, empathy, and many other complex things. The most powerful emotion we experience is love. Love is the emotion that drives us to do stupid and heroic things. It propels us to selfish desperation or pushes us to self-sacrifice.

As humans, we are on a constant search for love and acceptance. I believe that is a very specific part of the way God created us. God made us with the desire for love, because it was essential that we search for Him. As believers—now that we have found Him—we need to accept His unconditional, all-powerful, all-encompassing, merciful, and gracious love for us. So many of our confidence problems come from the fact that we do not believe God. He tells us about His amazing love for us, but we don't think this kind of love is real. Our logical, sin-filled minds tell us that not even God could possibly love us the way God says He does. We need to switch off our sinful hearts and trust that God says what He means. Remember that God cannot lie (Titus 1:2), and let's look through some scriptures together.

"Behold what manner of love the Father has bestowed on us, that we should be called children of God! Therefore the world does not know us, because it did not know Him." -1 John 3:1

"But God, who is rich in mercy, because of His great love with which he loved us, even when we were dead in trespasses, made us alive together with Christ (by grace you have been saved), and raised us up together, and made us sit together in the heavenly places in Christ Jesus, that in the ages to come He might show us the exceeding riches of His grace in His kindness toward us in Christ Jesus." -Ephesians 2:4-7

"Of His own will He brought us forth by the word of truth, that we might be a kind of firstfruits of His creatures." - James 1:18

God loves you with such a great love. When He created you, He was so excited. He knew the what, the why, and the how of everything about you. He had already planned what you would look like. God knew the way your personality would make you different from others. Your Heavenly Father looked forward to how He would delight in your times together. In fact, before you were born, He had already planned your eternal future with Him in heaven. In order to be with you, because He is holy and you are a sinner, God had to be willing to separate Himself from His One and only Son. But He was willing, and Jesus died on the cross just for you. I will go more into that later, but I wanted to mention it here because it's a huge plot point in your relationship with God. It is the moment that God put everything on the line. I am going to ask you to do something extremely difficult, but please try.

I know that there have been people that let you down. At times, no one was there for you when you needed someone. Please, make a strong effort not to put the feelings you have in your heart left over from that neglect onto God. He was not the One who neglected you. He was there for you the entire time. Yet you need to be the one to invite your Heavenly Father into these situations in your life. He will never force His company, advice, or unending love on you. Did you know that God is jealous for your time and attention? It is a perfect, sinless, jealousy. He created you, and He has very strong feelings about how He wants to spend time with you. In 2 Corinthians 11:2, Paul talks about having a "godly jealousy," wanting to make sure that the church body in Corinth remained pure and dedicated to God since they represented the bride of Christ. God—in perfect jealousy—waits for you.

When I think back to my years as a young Christian, through failed attempts to walk boldly with my trust in God's love for me, I remember that the same thought passed endlessly through my mind: *But You can't hug me or kiss me, God. How can I feel loved when I can't have those things?* God did not take my challenge lightly. He painted the most amazing sunrises for me at rowing practice and would whisper things like, "I made that just for you." When I felt lonely or afraid, He was with me. His presence became tangible to me in a whole new way. I could feel His encouragement when I needed it. When I mourned, He mourned with me. He lovingly chastened me to make better choices. He brought me confident sisters in the faith who accepted and loved me. These women even gave me those hugs I had been wanting so desperately. Once my heart was open to all the ways God had tried to romance me, I could see His fingerprints all over my life. My difficulties did not go away, but I could feel God walk through each circumstance or trial with me. I had been so afraid of being rejected by everyone that I was unable to see that God had lovingly accompanied me through it all. But now that fear was gone.

Have you allowed yourself to see the ways that God cherishes and loves you? Have you been reading the love letters He wrote to you in His Word? Do you write back? How often do you talk to Him? I promise, He wants to hear from you more than you can understand right now. Do you have emotional needs, longings, and desires that you are scared will never be fulfilled? God wants to fill your heart to overflowing, but He is waiting for an invitation. In Jeremiah 31:13, God spoke to His people, Israel, *"Yes, I have loved you with an everlasting love; Therefore with lovingkindness I have drawn you."* That is also the way that God feels about you. He loves you with an everlasting love, and with lovingkindness He has attempted to draw you toward Himself. If you have been resisting, please stop. It is time to enter into the joy, confidence, and security that await the children of God who understand the fullness of His love for them.

"There is no fear in love; but perfect love casts out fear, because fear involves torment. But he who fears has not been made perfect in love." -1 John 4:18

These verses all come together to form an amazing picture of the type of esteem we've searched for and needed all along: as His children we are God-esteemed.

GOD'S CREATIVE CREATION

As we discussed in Chapter 3, there is an unfortunate

link in our minds between our physical appearance and our ability to be loved. If we don't look, dress, or style ourselves according to an ever-changing standard set by random strangers that decide what's popular at the moment, then no one will ever choose to love us. That is not the way God sees things. In fact, His process is quite the opposite. He created you the exact way that you are because He loves you. Now that we have talked about God's love for us, it is time to discuss how His love for us is displayed through the way He created us, inside and out.

We need to discuss our dissatisfaction about our physical appearances. This may not to be an easy thing to discuss, but I promise that this will be one of the most healing conversations you have ever had. Everything that is broken must be brought to the light of truth before it can be properly healed.

You and I were both created by God. Sometimes, I think we forget that. If we do, that is the first way we fall into the trap Satan has set for us. Satan wants us to feel worthless. If we remember that God carefully considered our make up, lovingly crafted us, and purposefully gave us everything we need to accomplish the mission He has given us personally, then we will not feel worthless or unloved. We need to deliberately put scriptures in our hearts to battle against the lies of Satan. God made us, and that makes us very valuable to our Heavenly Father.

"For we are His workmanship, created in Christ Jesus for good works, which God prepared beforehand that we should walk in them." -Ephesians 2:10

If I'm honest, I'll admit that for a long time I hated this Bible verse. I thought it was cliché and could not imagine how so many women used this verse to understand their beauty. *Maybe it makes you feel beautiful to write this verse all over your house, and teach it countless times, but it doesn't make me feel any better. It doesn't apply to me*, I thought. Now, having been given wisdom and discernment from the Lord, I look at this statement and recognize its bitterness. God hadn't made me the way I thought He should have, and I was bitter toward Him because of that. Anytime you hear a Bible verse and start to feel angry you should examine your heart for bitterness toward God. What is the best way to get rid of bitterness? To humble yourself before the Lord, understand that He knows best, and repent. Say you're sorry and ask for forgiveness. Now that the sincere repentance has washed the bitterness out of my heart, I can see that God was telling the truth the entire time. I am a beautiful and unique creation of His, crafted to do the things He planned for my life, if I should choose to follow Him. Let's look at a few more verses to tuck away in our hearts, so we can defend against those fiery arrows of deception that Satan will inevitably shoot at us.

"I will praise You, for I am fearfully and wonderfully made; Marvelous are Your works, and that my soul knows very well. My frame was not hidden from You, when I was made in secret, and skillfully wrought in the lowest parts of the earth. Your eyes saw my substance, being yet unformed. And in Your book they all were written, the days fashioned for me, when as yet there were none of them. How precious also are Your thoughts to me, O God! How great is the sum of them!" –Psalm 139:14-17

"But the very hairs of your head are all numbered." – Matthew 10:30

Maybe you need a Bible verse to soften your heart toward God. Have you been feeling bitter toward the Lord because of the way He created you or due to unpleasant circumstances? God loves you so much that He keeps your tears in a bottle! How can you stay angry at Someone who loves you so dearly? The Bible says in Psalm 56:8, *"You number my wanderings; put my tears into Your bottle; Are they not in Your book?"* But perhaps, like me, even after all those truths, encouragements, and outpourings of love, you are still angry. There is one more thing I want to share with you about God's love.

Back at the Park

Let's rewind back to the second chapter. I was at the playground with my two daughters, and several other mothers were there with their children as well. As I watched the girls run around, I looked at the different mothers. At that point, my heart had been constantly hammered by feelings of worthlessness and I felt desperate. I cried out to God for understanding. "Lord," I prayed, "If You don't help me understand Your plan for my life, I am going to lose my mind. Why did You command me to tell people about You, and then make me have this personality and appearance? I am going to fail! And I am going to mess up my kids if things keep going this way. Please, help me?"

I think God had been waiting patiently for me to break. This was the turning point in my journey to attaining godly confidence. God had been wanting to tell me about His plan, but until that moment I had not been ready to believe Him. His answer to my prayer was, "Your low self-esteem is actually pride. Will you repent?" I felt sick to my stomach. He was right. After all that time spent in self-pity and operating out of self-protection, I could see my sin and it was disgusting. I asked God for forgiveness right then and there, and the most amazing thing happened. Once I allowed God to purge my heart of the wicked sin of pride, He showed me something I suspect He had wanted to show me all along.

I remember looking at each different woman around the playground (remember, there were only women there, that doesn't mean God feels differently about men). One was thin, another medium build, and yet another was plus-sized. As I looked at each different woman, God gave me a vision of a different flower. Each flower was a perfect match for the different body type of each woman. Then God showed me a field of flowers. I heard His subtle whisper in my heart, "How boring would it be if every flower was the same?" I saw visions of every flower on earth as a daisy, my favorite flower. But when there was not another type of flower anywhere, the daisy became boring and lost its unique beauty. God whispered one final thing, "Why wouldn't I give the same individual attention to each person? You are My flowers."

Pan over to me as tears ran down my face while I attempted to avoid the ugly cry. Perhaps the strangers around me attributed the tears to my very pregnant condition. No one said anything to me. I tear up now as I'm writing this. You, dear child of God, are His flower. He has created you, and you are wonderful. Stop the pointless comparison between roses and daisies! They are each special and beautiful in their own ways. End the senseless expectation that your physical appearance must fit within the constraints of worldly assumptions. God never meant for you to think that way. He created you the exact way you are for His glory and His purpose. I'm a peony, and you're a snapdragon. That's the way it's supposed to be. Let's all stand together and strive to understand what real beauty we create, as a special and beloved part of God's colorful and diverse bouquet. God took the time to make you one of a kind because He loves and cherishes you. To Him, you couldn't be more wonderfully unique. You are God-esteemed.

For The Fellas

As I was thinking about the second edition of this book, I asked God to give me a less feminine illustration, just in case some of my brothers don't really feel connected to the idea of being symbolized by a flower in a bouquet. He brought me to Abraham's story.

"Then He brought him outside and said, 'Look now toward heaven, and count the stars if you are able to number them.' And He said to him, 'So shall your descendants be.'" –Genesis 15:5

Stars. There are more than we could ever hope to count. And they have so many ways in which they vary: the number of atoms they posses; brightness (or luminescence); color; surface temperature; size (some are huge like our sun, others are relatively tiny); mass; and motion. Because of all these variables, the probability of having two totally identical stars is zero (similar to snowflakes). These unique creations are scattered throughout the hundreds of billions of galaxies in our physical universe. Yet, our Heavenly Father took the time to create each individual star, just as He purposefully created you. Next time you feel worthless or generic, think about the stars.

AT THE CROSS

There is one more aspect I want to talk about in regard to God's personal love for you. Write this profound truth on your heart and purpose never to forget it.

"But God demonstrates His own love toward us, in that while we were still sinners, Christ died for us." –Romans 5:8

Jesus died on the cross for you. God loves you so much that He made the ultimate sacrifice. God is holy— He literally cannot be in the presence of unrighteousness in heaven—so He had to send His Son to save you.

"Therefore do not be ashamed of the testimony of our Lord, nor of me His prisoner, but share with me in the sufferings for the gospel according to the power of God, who

has saved us and called us with a holy calling, not according to our works, but according to His own purpose and grace which was given to us in Christ Jesus before time began, but now has been revealed by the appearing of our Savior Jesus Christ, who has abolished death and brought life and immortality to light through the gospel." -2 Timothy 1:8-10

He has saved us and called us with a holy calling. God has loved you since before time began. He is the hero in this story, and we are the ones that need to be rescued.

I love comic books, and in every compelling comic book character arc, there is that moment where the hero has to be willing to give up everything in order to save the person that he cares about the most. If God is the comic book hero, then you, the bride of Christ, are the one that God is willing to risk it all for. If you have waited for a more epic love story, it is not going to happen. God loved you in a way that compelled Him to send His Son to Earth to die. Jesus gave His life for yours on the cross. When you are tempted to believe the lie that you are worthless, remember that God gave everything just to be with you.

"For God so loved the world that He gave His only begotten Son, that whoever believes in Him should not perish but have everlasting life." -John 3:16

PRACTICAL APPLICATION

By now, I hope that the power of God's love and the fact that He purposefully made you collectively blows your mind. At this point, you may wonder, "How can I use this knowledge to change my attitude, actions, and thoughts?" That, dear friend, is an excellent question.

The most important thing you can do is to decide that you are no longer going to believe Satan's lies. Start to memorize scripture to use to defend against the enemy when he whispers those deceptive thoughts. At the beginning of the book I mentioned a giveaway that includes a list of all of the Bible verses used in each chapter along with some cool printables you can hang up in your house. You can use this list and the printables as tools to equip your mind to put up a righteous front as you encounter spiritual warfare. As I have been putting together this book, I have been plagued by lies nearly every time I look in the mirror. In my thoughts, I have heard the hiss of accusations like, "Look at you! You're so fat and ugly! How can YOU possibly write a book about godly confidence. You hypocrite!" But I know none of those things are true. They are lies, and I have the scriptures written on my heart to prove it. I have made it a point not to believe lies. As soon as these kinds of thoughts pop into my head, I kick them out. I refuse to dwell on them. I judge every thought according to this scripture found in Philippians 4:8, *"Finally, brethren, whatever things are true, whatever things are noble, whatever things are just, whatever things are pure, whatever things are lovely, whatever things are of good report, if there is any virtue and if there is anything praiseworthy—meditate on these things."*

If something comes into my mind and I wonder if I should think about it, I go down the list mentally, *"True, noble, just, pure, lovely, good report, virtuous, or praiseworthy."* If it doesn't fit under one of those categories, out it goes. Mentally, we must be prepared for spiritual battle.[1]

No matter what body type you have, there will be

---

[1] In the sequel to this book, *Confident Nobody*, I explain how to use questions to create victory in your thought life, even if Satan is using another person to put destructive thoughts in your mind.

temptation to view yourself through the lens of worldly expectations. You can build a defense against that using Philippians 4:8 as well. It could be that you are thin and you don't have any emphasis in the places that the world tells you that you should. Perhaps you aren't athletically built, or people say you're too athletic in build. In either case, there may be a temptation to get surgical alterations to your body, but that won't make you feel more secure.

If you are in the robust category, like me, the deception you hear is that you have too many curves in all the wrong places. People may assume you eat horribly and never exercise. Oh well, let them. I am careful about making healthy choices and work out several times a week, yet I am still a size 16. Yes, I just told you my size. I don't care who knows it, because this is how God created me. I wasn't supposed to be a size 6, or whatever else. I'm a size 16, just the way God planned for me to be. I also have friends that have had really great success with weight loss plans and programs that use pre-made food, but that just isn't for me. If this whole ordeal is really about being healthy, then I don't care about being skinny. That is not my goal. No matter what category you fit under, it comes down to one thing: Do you believe God when He says that He made you a specific way with a specific purpose in mind? Either you trust Him, or you don't. It is a choice that only you can make.

God Has Already Decided

Even if you look exactly the way the world wants you to, there will always be moments of deception where you feel too small in one area, or too large in another. It could be that you think your feet look weird, or your fingers are fluffy. I have chubby fingers, which is something I accept, although I still don't understand God's reasoning on that particular choice. I also have to wear corrective lenses if I want to see things clearly. Again, I don't understand God's choice, but I accept it. That's the point; I don't have to understand, but I need to choose to believe that God has His reasons. The same thing is true for all of us. You may not understand God's plan for your physical body, but He promises that there is one.

God also assures us all that we are beautifully and creatively made. Remember the pattern God gave us in Chapter 4 for dealing with insecurities? If we want to live in victory over them, we must choose to believe what God says. We also need to share our insecurities with Him so He can heal them. Imagine all of the amazing things God has been waiting to do through our lives once we have gained victory in this area.

I once read a book about how to heal after your husband has confessed to a pornography addiction. Many things in the book were helpful, but there was one thing at the end that bothered me long after I finished reading that book. The author shares that when she learned about her husband's pornography addiction, it made her more aware of her own insecurities, which I relate to. She mentions that in the past she used to spend two hours a day putting on makeup and doing her hair. In fact, she writes that she previously felt so uncomfortable letting her husband see her without makeup on, she would wake up way before he did just to put it on. At the end of the book, when she talks about being delivered from her insecurities, she mentions how she took all of the mirrors out of her house, leaving only one. The sole mirror left in her house is specially made so that when she looks at her own reflection, she has to look through a transposed image of Jesus Christ. That doesn't sound like true deliverance to me. If you cannot stand to look at yourself without being tempted to fall back into the temptation to alter your appearance with two hours worth of hair and makeup, you have not accepted that God created you to look and be a certain way. I share this in order to encourage you not to settle for less than God has in store for you. God wants to deliver you fully and completely from the deception that you are not a purposeful and wonderful creation. Pray for God to help you see yourself the way that He sees you—as a cherished and adored child. Pray to God for help and He will answer. If you still cannot stand to see your own reflection, you have not been fully delivered.

ENTROPY: KEEPING THINGS REAL SINCE THE FALL OF MAN

The next thing we need to address is entropy. Order must always decrease. No matter what you do, entropy is here to stay. So let's deal with it, shall we?

It could be that you have started to notice wrinkles and gray hair upon your person. At the writing of this book, I am 31, and I can find both (and now at 35 for the updated version I can find even more). I remember suffering a slight panic when I was pregnant with my youngest child as I noticed a selection of several gray hairs accumulating on my head. Then I remembered that I like gray hair, and credited the panic to overflowing pregnancy hormones. We are all aging as we grow closer to our bodies dying. There is nothing that can alter that progression. Still, that does not mean that we must despise this process.

The Bible says that, *"The glory of young men is their strength, and the splendor of old men is their gray head,"* in Proverbs 20:29. You may be strong when you are young, but if you have gray hair that means that you have had a long life and had many opportunities to grow. Would I trade all my smile lines and random gray hairs for the wisdom God has shared with me over the years? What if I could have my 20 year-old face and body back? To me, it would not be worth it. No way. Absolutely not. The longer you live, age, and follow after God, the more beautiful your inner-self gets. We waste so much time in anxiety over how our flesh appears. We should attempt to stay healthy by eating nutritious food and exercising, but in the end our flesh is still going to pass away. Only our spirits will remain. If we were to think logically, in light of the truth, we would focus all of our beauty treatments on our spirits.

"For if you live according to the flesh you will die; but if by the Spirit you put to death the deeds or the body, you will live." -Romans 8:13

Perhaps pregnancy has dramatically altered your body. I understand. I am there right now. My body is stretched and misshapen. I cannot avoid the "muffin top" appearance over the edge of my jeans unless I wear a brace to suck in the extra skin and temporarily correct my painful abdominal separation (which I have done physical therapy treatments for, but will eventually require surgery to correct). What we need to realize is that our bodies will deteriorate. We live in a fallen world, and our bodies age and decay. I can say without a doubt that God had a different plan for childbirth and how our bodies would react before Adam and Eve sinned in the Garden of Eden. However, that no longer applies to us.

As Christians, we have to accept that our bodies change. My kids point at the stretch marks that cover my stomach, hips, and the insides of my thighs, and comment about how strange they look. They mention that Mommy has extra skin and is a bit floppy in some places. These are the kind of honest observations children make out loud. I could respond in a defensive way, confirming their pre-formed ideas that every body should look a certain way, or I can share truth with them. I remind them that Mommy's body carried three babies full term, and even though it left my body looking a bit different, it was worth the change. They take turns and point to the different stretch marks. They make comments about which child made which mark. They think it's a fun game, and I cannot help but take joy in these moments. I relish the touch of little hands on the marks of my belly, and think about how I used to be able to feel their kicks inside of me before they were born. I remind them that not every body is supposed to look the same—that would be boring—and God doesn't make boring things. I make sure to tell them that when they are talking to people other than Mommy and Daddy, they need to keep these observations to themselves. We explain these observations may hurt someone's feelings if the children say them out loud. When it is just the family, we talk about how bodies will be different. If my daughters ever choose to have their own children, I want them to understand that these changes are normal, and that they do not need to have negative feelings about them. Men's bodies also change as they get older, and we need to prepare our sons and younger brothers for the aging process.

Has anyone ever had that conversation with you? If not, I suspect it was because the men and women in your life were struggling with their own insecurities. So let's have that conversation right now, shall we? It is okay for your body to change. The extra skin, extra weight, or stretch marks are okay (men get stretch marks, too, by the way). They really are. You are still you, and you are still just as magnificent as ever. You are still a beautiful creation and loved child of our Lord and King. Having a few scars or memory marks on your flesh does not change how God feels about you. He still loves you just as much as He always has. Don't give into the unrealistic expectations that the world and Satan have about your aging and changing body. They want to steal your joy and make you discontent, but you can choose how you respond. You can choose to say, "No, I won't let Satan and worldly influences win. I choose to believe God. I know that He will help me get through these changes. He loves me and says that I am exquisite."

"Enter by the narrow gate; for wide is the gate and broad is the way that leads to destruction, and there are many who go in by it. Because narrow is the gate and difficult is the way which leads to life, and there are few who find it." - Matthew 7:13-14

Jesus used this parable as a clear illustration for salvation, however, I also think that these verses create a valuable illustration for the kind of Christian life we can choose. I would like to reexamine this parable and think of it in terms of our journey throughout our Christian lives, and I want to end this chapter with a reminder of the choice you have before you.

My dear and beloved brother or sister, you can choose to believe God. That is the narrow path. It is full of difficulties. On this road, you will have to protect yourself with every spiritual piece of armor you can find, but you will feel loved and adored. This path will lead you to understand God's love for you in an entirely new way. Like Mrs. Thirsty, you will find spiritual fulfillment. In contrast, you can also refuse to believe God. You can choose to ignore the truth that God lovingly placed in the Bible for you. The path in the other direction is wide, full of deception, desperation, and emptiness. On this road, you will have plenty of company, but everyone there will be miserable. When you choose this path, you will forfeit the amazing plan God has for your life, and you will never experience the spiritual fulfillment Mrs. Thirsty found in Jesus Christ. You can choose to hold onto the lie that you are a mistake, but I pray that you would choose to believe

God, and take the narrow path. I have lived on the wide path, clutching tightly to my pride and the belief that God made me worthless. It is empty and leads to bitterness. I want to warn you against this kind of life, but in the end, it is your choice. It is God's will for you to avoid the pain associated with these lies and the emptiness that follows.

* * *

YOUR PERSONAL JOURNEY

Sometimes, even after seeing all the proof of God's love, God's plan for every individual life, and God's care during difficult circumstances, people still struggle to accept that their insecurities are based on lies that oppose God's word. If you find that you are still struggling to accept that God didn't make any mistakes when He created you, it could be that you need to dig deeper into your own personal story to determine why you feel that way. There are extra steps you may need to take in order to further combat false ideas and lies that have now become a normal way of thinking. Let's talk about exploring your personal story.

Your Story

When we go through difficult or traumatic experiences in our lives, often, our minds will block out certain memories as a way of dealing with them so that we can continue to function.

One of the reasons that you have found it difficult to find deliverance from your insecurities may be that you still haven't been able to remember all of the reasons why you feel so insecure. There are several questions you can work through to determine if this is the case in your situation. It is best to read them over, think about them for several days, and then discuss your answers

with a trusted friend and/or counselor.
   Let's look at the questions.

   -What are the most intense insecurities you
   experience? Make a list of your most powerful
   insecurities. Be as specific as possible.

   -Can you remember when you started feeling
   each specific insecurity? Write down the earliest
   memory you have of each individual insecurity.

   -Is there a specific person that you associate
   with your feelings of worthlessness? Take some
   time to think about the way that person's
   behavior has shaped the way you feel.

   -When are you most vulnerable to your
   insecurities? It could be that there are certain
   triggers that have formed because of past
   instances of verbal abuse or lack of support from
   a loved one. Have you ever experienced a person
   in your life repeatedly telling you something
   negative about your appearance or personality? It
   could be that things that remind you of that
   person trigger stronger feelings of insecurity.
   For example, perhaps your great aunt always
   told you how she thought you were unattractive.
   When you see things that remind you of your
   aunt, or hear things that are similar to what she
   said, it might bring back the feelings of
   inadequacy that you associate with having been

around her.

-Are there any pivotal moments in your life that have shaped your feelings of worthlessness? Have you ever discussed these events with a close friend, mentor, or counselor? If not, I strongly encourage you to do so. It will help you work through these emotions so that you can work toward healing.

Confronting the Truth

In many situations, until we confront the false ideas and impressions that have been made on us throughout our lives, we cannot accept the truth that God's word tells us about our value as His children. It is time for us to have those confrontations. We must refuse to let Satan steal more of our time: that is exactly what he wants. I am not saying that this journey down memory lane will be painless. People that have felt worthless are often in a great deal of pain. Real healing for this specific pain can only come through praying, learning of important biblical truths, and experiencing an intense season of personal grief. However, I strongly believe that this process is worth the end result.

CHAPTER 7

EARTHLY PARENTS AND OUR HEAVENLY FATHER

Often, when I talk to someone about their confidence issues, one of the first things that comes up is some issue they have with one or both parents. I have personally experienced a lot of heartache regarding my own relationships with each of my parents. It is difficult to separate our ideas about our earthly parents from our

Father in heaven, even though we must. On one hand, earthly parents are human and they sin. They will never be perfect and they can never fill the God-shaped holes in our hearts. On the other hand, God has entrusted us to our parents, and commanded them to teach us about Him.

"And you, fathers, do not provoke your children to wrath, but bring them up in the training and admonition of the Lord." -Ephesians 6:4

As a parent, I take this responsibility very seriously. I do my best to be a godly example and teach my kids everything that the Bible teaches, but I also teach my children that their mommy (me) will fail—moms sin, too, and will sometimes let their children down. But God never fails, He never sins, and He will never let His kids down.

The goal of this chapter is to help us separate the feelings and expectations we have for our earthly parents from the ones we have for our Heavenly Father. We will discuss some common parent-related issues and how these problems affect our ideas about personal confidence. It is also important to examine how to forgive our earthly parents for any areas in which they may have fallen short of God's commands to raise us in the knowledge of Him, or to love us the way He does.

There is nothing that a small child desires more than the knowledge that they are loved. Over fifty years ago, in any town in any state in the United States, Satan thought he had won a very important battle. He made it a cultural stigma for fathers to tell their children that they loved them. Even the most loving men gave into the lie that it was shameful to verbally admit their parental love, though they had no problem stating their love for their country or favorite sports team. Can you imagine what it would be like to grow up never hearing your father tell you that he loved you? I know that some of you experienced this horrible cultural phenomenon, and I'm sorry. That was never God's plan. Why would Satan wage such a battle?

When parents, especially fathers, do not tell their children that they love and accept them, bad things happen. Damaged men and women, on their quest to feel some type of love and acceptance, embrace drugs, sex, and empty solutions to their soul problems. I don't think Satan, with all his worldly knowledge, saw the Jesus movement coming in the 1970s, but it did. The weapon God used to destroy Satan's tactic to make a generation of children feel unloved was the overflowing love of Jesus Christ. This was an interesting time in Christian history for the United States, and I think that it brings to light an interesting concept. In earlier chapters, we established that God created us with the desire to feel loved. When individuals do not feel loved, broken hearts lead to bitter souls.

Following Job's Example

One of the easiest ways for Satan to attack an individual is by creating tension or apathy in their family unit. That is the exact way of attack Satan takes when God gives him permission to test the God-fearing man, Job. Let me set the scene for you. God is having a conversation with Satan, and God points to Job. God calls Job a faithful servant and Satan makes a comment about how much God has blessed Job with. Satan says that as soon as God removes the blessings, that Job will curse God to His face. In response, God tells Satan to do whatever he wants to do to Job, as long as Satan doesn't kill Job. Suddenly, all of Job's land is taken, and his servants and animals are killed by raiders.

Then Job gets even worse news in Job 1:18, *"While he was still speaking, another also came and said, "Your sons and daughters were eating and drinking wine in their oldest brother's house, and suddenly a great wind came from across the wilderness and struck the four corners of the house, and it fell on the young people, and they are dead; and I alone have escaped to tell you!"* Up until this point, Job is okay. We don't read about any reaction until after he hears about his children. In response, he tears his robe, shaves his head, and then falls to the ground to worship the Lord. I often marvel at Job's response, because I don't know if I would respond so righteously in the same situation. If Job wasn't so faithful and disciplined in his relationship with the Lord, things could have gone much differently. If Job didn't understand God's love for him as an individual, he could have fallen apart. Dear friend, that is exactly what Satan is counting on the rest of us to do—fall apart. Job's wife did; she told her husband to curse God and die. We should want to be like Job, not like his wife.

Generational Curses and Other Complications

If you haven't ever felt loved by your parents, I am sorry. I think God would want me to tell you that. He gave your parents the ability to make their own choices, and parents are sinful people, like everyone else on this planet. Perhaps your parents did tell you that they loved you, but they did not make you feel loved. Maybe they made you feel worthless with their unrealistic expectations, harsh words, or lack of physical affection. It is very likely that your parents tried to break the bad pattern they experienced as children, but failed. In the Old Testament we see that bad familial habits transcend generations.

"And the Lord passed before him and proclaimed, 'The Lord, the Lord God, merciful and gracious, longsuffering, and abounding in goodness and truth, keeping mercy for thousands, forgiving iniquity and transgression and sin, by no means clearing the guilty, visiting the iniquity of the fathers upon the children and children's children to the third and fourth generation." -Exodus 34:6-7

God is quick to forgive at any time, but, in this chunk

of scripture, we also see that bad habits (iniquities) like worshipping other gods, will be passed down from one family member to another. Many families are caught in this trap, and need to turn to God and stop worshipping idols if they want to be free from this evil inheritance. If you have experienced a painful childhood, God is the only one that will deliver you from it. You cannot overcome these obstacles on your own. Repent from the sins that are accepted and even admired in your family. This is the only way to break free from the bondage that has kept generations of your loved ones confined and condemned.

It might be that one or both parents have died. I am so sorry for your loss if this has happened to you. I won't begin to pretend that I know the feelings you have about this, because I have not experienced them[2]. But I can direct you to the Lord. He truly understands and He wants to be there to support you during your grief. Talk to Him. Tell Him everything. I promise, He is listening and He wants to hear what you have to say. Remember, this is the same God that stores your tears in a bottle.

OVERCOMING PARENTAL NEGATIVITY AND NEGLECT

---

[2] Upon writing the updated version of this book, I have watched my husband go through the unexplainable loss of his beloved father due to complications resulting from a skiing accident. I will say there is no pain quite like knowing that someone you love so dearly is no longer on Earth. I have chronicled part of our journey as a grieving family in *Confident Nobody*.

We often view our parents as mini-gods, associating our worth with our perception of how our parents view us. If they seem dissatisfied with our abilities and choices, God must be as well. If they are loving and approve of our choices, then God does too. This is not reality. First, God always loves you, no matter what your parents say. Second, your parents may approve of choices you make that contradict the Word of God. The Bible does say that we should obey our parents (Ephesians 6:1), but it does not say that we should choose to please our parents over pleasing God. In Acts 5:29, we read that *"We ought to obey God rather than men."* Without someone to remind of us of God's love for us and to teach us what the Bible says, we often live our lives in search of acceptance, especially from our parents. I have often heard this phrase, "I was never good enough for..." and enter either "my father," or "my mother." I think this is something we need to talk about in the light of the truth of God's word.

Parents are men and women, children of God, and they are capable of making foolish choices. I am at a point in my life where I am determined not to let my parents' opinions matter more to me than God's. I am not saying that I am disrespectful to my parents. I know that it is God's will for me to be respectful and to honor my parents (Exodus 20:12). But I must not agree with them if I feel like they have told me to do something unbiblical. In addition, I must choose not to take the things they say as personal attacks, even if they are. But why? Why should I give my parents grace and mercy if they fail to be the godly examples in my life that I wish they would be?

The Wicked Man

I don't want to be like "the wicked man" we read about in Psalm 109:16.

"Because he did not remember to show mercy, but

persecuted the poor and needy man, that he might even slay the broken in heart."

As I prayed about my parents, their influence in my life, and all of the hurts from the past, I asked God to help me see my parents the way that He sees them. May I suggest to you that your parents are brokenhearted and in need of mercy? I understand what it is like to be taught that you are not good enough. It hurts.

But let me ask you a question: have you ever thought about why your parents act the way they do? Have you ever tried looking at them the way that God looks at them? It could be that when God looks down on your mother or father, He sees a broken little child in need of a Heavenly Father to love and chasten them. However, everyone, including parents, will be held responsible for their choices. We all need to repent from sin and follow after Jesus' example. In the meantime, it is God's desire for you to forgive them and show them mercy. I know this is a difficult thing to ask, but God never asks you to do things in your own strength.

"Therefore I take pleasure in infirmities, in reproaches, in necessities, in persecutions, in distresses for Christ's sake: for when I am weak, then I am strong." -2 Corinthians 12:10

When Paul the Apostle said this, he meant that God works in our weakness to show us and others His strength. When we are weak and God helps us, He gets all the glory. There are many situations that will be too difficult for us to face on our own, and that is when we need to ask God for His help. To forgive others that have hurt us emotionally is very difficult, but God promises that He will complete every good work He has begun in us. This is a concept that we will need to repeat over and over in our walks with Jesus Christ, because forgiveness, especially within the context of a complex relationship like a familial one, is a process. It isn't something we do once and then forget. We have to choose to forgive every time the temptation to become bitter over a difficult memory arises.

"Being confident of this very thing, that He who has begun a good work in you will complete it until the day of Jesus Christ." –Philippians 1:6

THE CYCLE CONTINUES

When broken, hurt people have their own children, the cycle of destructive behavior usually passes from one generation to another. In order to understand God and Satan's respective roles in the way family dynamics play out, let's take a look at two different situations in parenthood that are unfortunately common.

Isabelle is suddenly a single mother who went through a nasty divorce when her husband left her for a younger woman. Even though she never felt fulfilled in her marital relationship, now she feels even more vulnerable and dejected. Despite her bitterness toward men and romantic relationships, she still feels that there must be someone who can make her feel loved and appreciated. Isabelle has two young children that have instantly become her life. She spends all of her time and energy on them. In return, she expects them to meet her emotional needs. Whenever something is wrong, she forces them to snuggle with her, and tells them about all of her fears and struggles. What her kids really need—to feel their mother's unconditional love— is in direct contrast to Isabelle's very conditional love. Her children correctly perceive that their mother will only love them if they bear her emotional burdens. Over time they crumble under the pressure, and the cycle of unloved feelings flows from one generation into the next.

As a somewhat successful business owner, Bill has failed to become the doctor that his father always wanted him to be. Bill's father is cordial, but has never told Bill that he loves him. There is a giant hole in Bill's heart where his father's approval would fit, but it will never be given. As the years go by, their relationship becomes more strained and Bill becomes distant. Slowly, Bill starts a family of his own, unable to shake the idea that if one of his children becomes a doctor, he will finally earn his father's approval. Even though his daughter shows a natural gift for painting and drawing, he pushes her toward math and science. Instead of doing what is best for her individually, Bill pressures his daughter to become a doctor. He refuses to give her the acceptance she longs for unless she submits to his will. This destructive cycle has become a family legacy that continues until Bill's daughter stops talking to him altogether. When she doesn't ask him to walk her down the aisle at her wedding, the hole in his heart turns into a canyon of despair and pain.

These are two examples of the many ways that Satan deceives parents in an attempt to get them to seriously damage their children. He has parents all over the world convinced that their children somehow possess the answer to filling the emptiness that defines their lives, even though their children never will. If you are a parent, I want to share something with you: no matter what your children do or don't do, whether they love you or not, they will never be able to give you the spiritual fulfillment you are looking for. Only Jesus Christ can fill that longing you have, and take that emptiness away forever. By attempting to fulfill your personal needs through your children, you will damage them and continue in the generational chain of brokenness that you never wanted to participate in. God commands us to love others unconditionally, and that especially applies to our children. When you attach your personal value to your child's actions, ambitions, and affections, you pass down all of the broken-heartedness that you vowed you would end. If you are doing this to your child, stop right now. Don't let Satan manipulate you for one more second. Pray for God's forgiveness and ask your children for their forgiveness as well.

If you have been a victim of this type of parenting, there can still be healing. Remember God's love for you —He is near to the brokenhearted (Psalm 34:18). Let God comfort you and ask Him to heal your heart.

"But God, who is rich in mercy, because of His great love with which He loved us, even when we were dead in trespasses, made us alive together with Christ (by grace you have been saved)." -Ephesians 2:4-5

God loves us with a great love and He is rich in mercy. Write these words on your heart and don't forget them. Even if your parent has never shown you this kind of unconditional love, God has. He is the one who has made you alive in Jesus Christ—no earthly parent can undo that.

The only way to battle against bitterness in your life is to forgive. If you want peace from the hurts and unrealistic expectations of your parents, you must forgive them. This is a process that needs to happen continually.

At one point in my life I made the decision that I would forgive my parents for all past and future hurts (if your parent has a pattern of offensive behavior, that won't change unless they do). My new approach is to choose to hold onto all of the positive things my parents have done along with the valuable lessons they have taught me. If I teach my own children God's word and the positive parts of the lessons I learned from my parents, I am allowing God to transform the negative legacy I inherited into something infinitely better: God's holy plan for my family. Whenever I am tempted to dwell on past hurts, I remember Ephesians 4:31-32, *"Let all bitterness, wrath, anger, clamor, and evil speaking be put away from you, with all malice. And be kind to one another, tenderhearted, forgiving one another, even as God in Christ forgave you."*

OUR HEAVENLY FATHER

"But as many as received Him, to them He gave the right to become children of God, to those who believe in His name." -John 1:12

Is it disappointing to admit that your earthly parents have failed or will fail you? Yes, I think it is only natural to feel sad when we find out that our parents are not the superheroes we had imagined them to be. Instead of growing bitter about this, we can learn to show our parents love, forgiveness, and mercy, while embracing God as our Heavenly Father. Our Lord and Heavenly Father will never stop loving us. He will never fail and His mercy endures forever (Psalm 136). There are four main areas of fathering with which God provides His children. We crave these things from our earthly parents as well, but even the most godly parents can never meet the deepest needs we feel to belong to someone the same way that God can.

HE REACHES OUT

In our relationship with God, He is the one that risks His heart. We know that He will always love and accept us, but the opposite is not guaranteed. Just look at the nation of Israel in the Old Testament. How many times did God welcome the people back into His care to be rejected yet again? God sets Himself up for repeated heartbreak just to have the opportunity to have a relationship with us.

We read in 1 John 4:19 that, *"We love Him because He first loved us."* God is the one who is constantly putting His feelings at risk in this relationship. Yet, many of the people in this world still reject Him and His Son, Jesus Christ. Even when we make bad choices, or make God angry, He still chooses to love us. But why? In 1 John 3:1-2 we see God reaching out to us, *"Behold what manner of love the Father has bestowed on us, that we should be called children of God! Therefore the world does not know us, because it did not know Him. Beloved, now we are children of God; and it has not yet been revealed what we shall be, but we know that when He is revealed, we shall be like Him, for we shall see Him as He is."* The first thing I want to point out is that God loves His children. In fact, the very act of being called "children of God" is a way that God gives us His love. Conversely, because we are His children, He loves us. Because of this love, God has given us the amazing gift of salvation. He has pardoned the punishment we deserve for our sins and exchanged it for eternal life with Him.

He has also given us His Word—not because He has some insane standard for us to live up to so that we might earn His love—but so that we would live the best life possible. He knows everything, and He wanted to share that wisdom with us. You cannot earn God's love. That is not the point of the Bible. The point of God's Word—an amazing instruction guide that teaches us how to have a fruitful and faithful life—is to help us along on our journey toward eternity, and to equip us to take as many people with us as we possibly can. It is **not** a guidebook of how to do stuff that will make God love us. Remember Romans 6:23, which says that salvation is a gift. *"For the wages of sin is death, but the gift of God is eternal life in Christ Jesus our Lord."* God already loves us, and that isn't going to change no matter what we do.

Something I always tell my children is, "Mommy may not like the choices you make sometimes, but I will always love you." I hate it when my kids make choices that I know will harm them in the long run: whether it is greed, unforgiveness, or a rebellious heart. But, I always love them. It is this love for them that causes me to have a broken heart when I see them headed for their own heart break. This is the same way God feels about us, but with a perfect, supernatural love. If God's love for us is based on our ability to work our way into His approval, then He is no better than our earthly, sinful parents.

"...that the world may know that You have sent Me, and have loved them as You have loved Me. Father, I desire that they also whom You gave Me may be with Me where I am, that they may behold My glory which You have given Me; for You loved Me before the foundation of the world." –John 17:23b–24

Listen, Jesus says that God loved Him before the foundation of the world. Jesus also says that God loves us as He loves Jesus. This means that God has loved us since before the foundation of the world. I hope you are feeling loved right now, because His love for you began before the foundations of this world (Ephesians 1:4).

HE ADOPTS US

The second thing I want to address is that God has adopted us. He is our Father. The heavenly court documents have been approved and signed. I have seen friends go through tireless processes to be able to adopt precious children. And after their final day in court, what do you think they do? They celebrate because the child they knew was theirs all along is officially, legally theirs. This is the exact same way God feels about us.

It could be that you have a strained relationship with your earthly parents, or maybe they have passed away. When I was a teenager, I had a very unhealthy relationship with my earthly father. During one of the most difficult times in my life, I could not seek spiritual counsel from him. In fact, he would often provoke me into arguments that usually ended with me in tears. I knew that my earthly father was not going to help with my spiritual growth, so I turned to my Heavenly Father. In Psalm 68:5-6 it reads, *"A father to the fatherless, a defender of widows, is God in His holy habitation. God sets the solitary in families; He brings those who are bound into prosperity; But the rebellious will dwell in a dry land."* God will be a father to the fatherless. That encourages me so much. I hope it also encourages you.

Whether you have problems with your mother or your father, God is there for you. He promises to be the stable parent that you long for. Remember that God already loves you. His parental affection and approval can overcome any feelings of worthlessness or insufficiency that our earthly parents have caused. God can also bring brothers and sisters in the faith to be as close as our blood relatives, and sometimes even closer.

He sets the solitary in families, and that means that He can provide you with a spiritual family that shares your love of Jesus Christ and God's commandments. If you are lacking spiritual fellowship, get plugged into a Bible-teaching church. Join one of the smaller ministries that needs volunteers or ask someone in church leadership to help you find a small group. For introverts (like me), I know how challenging this can be, but God will bless your efforts.

HE PROVIDES FOR US

One thing that God has commanded fathers to do is to provide for the physical needs of their families. I am not saying that there will never be times of unemployment or financial struggles for believers, but what I am saying is that it is the duty of the parent to do their best to provide for their family. This doesn't mean that everyone in the family has a smartphone. It means their family has a place to sleep, food to eat, and, most importantly, is taught about God and His Word. Not all parents are able or willing to do these things, but once again, God has that aspect of His Father role covered.

"Or what man is there among you who, if his son asks for bread, will give him a stone? Or if he asks for a fish, will he give him a serpent? If you then, being evil, know how to give good gifts to your children, how much more will your Father who is in heaven give good things to those who ask Him!" - Matthew 7:9-11

Even evil people feel that they should give their children good gifts (of course many of us have also experienced how selfish ambitions can derail many parents from choosing to bless their children). God wants to provide so much more for us. He loves us and out of His perfect love for us He wants to bless us.

"Now this is the confidence that we have in Him, that if we ask anything according to His will, He hears us. And if we know that He hears us, whatever we ask, we know that we have the petitions that we have asked of Him." -1 John 5:14-15

"Consider the lilies, how they grow: they neither toil nor spin; and yet I say to you, even Solomon in all his glory was not arrayed like one of these. If then God so clothes the grass, which today is in the field and tomorrow is thrown into the oven, how much more will He clothe you, O you of little faith? And do not seek what you should eat or what you

should drink, nor have an anxious mind. For all these things the nations of the world seek after, and your Father knows that you need these things. But seek the kingdom of God, and all these things shall be added to you." –Luke 12:27-31

God cares for us, and promises that He will give us clothes and food. He promises that He hears us when we ask for things. The only reason God does not give us the specific things we want is when they are in contrast with His will for our lives. When we pray, our underlying prayer should be for God's will to be done. God knows everything and He knows what is best for us. My husband and I have gone through times of extreme dependence on God for things as simple as food and clothing. There were nights when we did not know what we would eat for dinner, as we were out of food and money (this is actually a fairly frequent experience among foreign missionaries when they first go out on the field). Miraculously, God would have someone drop by with a meal for us. This season taught us how fully we can depend on our Heavenly Father. He never let us go hungry, and at the same time He strengthened our faith by providing for each individual need, one at a time. One day my husband found money on the sidewalk so he could buy groceries. A different time I found some vegetables someone had dropped on the way home from the farmer's market. They were dirty, but I washed them off and cooked them. I would not trade those difficult days for anything. I can say without a doubt that God does provide. He may not give us things exactly the way we want them, but He always loves us and He does not forget about us or our physical needs.

HE TEACHES US

The last thing I want to talk about is how God the Father teaches His children.

"Now to Him who is able to keep you from stumbling, and to present you faultless before the presence of His glory with exceeding joy, to God our Savior, who alone is wise, be glory and majesty, dominion and power, both now and forever. Amen." -Jude 24-25

The first thing we see in this verse is that God never places unrealistic expectations on His children. He gives us the spiritual tools we need in order to help us accomplish His will. He is able to present us faultless before His presence because of what Jesus Christ accomplished on the cross, not because of anything we have done. The second thing we see is that God alone is wise. Unlike our earthly parents, God will never associate our successes or failures with His own worth. God is God, no matter how you and I perform in this life. God loves us unconditionally, and He does not put pressure on us the same way that earthly parents sometimes do.

God also allows us to have wisdom we would not otherwise have. The closer I get to the Lord, the more I understand in general. Remember what the Bible says about wisdom.

"The fear of the Lord is the beginning of wisdom; A good understanding have all those who do His commandments. His praise endures forever." -Psalm 111:10

When we fear God, He gives us better wisdom and understanding. Whether this teaching is about work situations, how to raise our children, how to choose a spouse, or how to serve others at church, God will expand our knowledge when we fear Him.

❖ ❖ ❖

RELATIONSHIP RESTORATION

Just because you have a difficult relationship with your parent now does not mean that will always be the case. Continue to pray for them and love them unconditionally, the way you would want them to love you. I have been very blessed to see my constant prayers for my father answered. He is now walking with the Lord, and God has done a lot of healing in my heart about the past. For many years I thought that my father would never return to a fruitful walk with the Lord, but I kept praying, because I knew that my continued praying would please the Lord. There were so many times when I felt like giving up, but I knew that no matter what my father chose to do, my prayers were pleasing to God. After over 10 years of fervent prayer, my father returned to his first love, Jesus Christ. Don't lose faith. Keep praying. Keep hoping. Remember that love hopes all things (1 Corinthians 13:7). If your parent passed away before reconciliation happened, there can still be restoration in your life. Find someone older in the faith who exhibits fruits of the spirit to counsel you. Talk through your childhood and the negative things that occurred in your relationship with your parents so that healing can begin. Pray and ask God to help you fully forgive your parent. Pray for God to show you how to give them the same grace and mercy that He has given you.

A NOTE TO THOSE WHO HAVE EXPERIENCED PHYSICAL OR EMOTIONAL TRAUMA

It is important to make a distinction about experiences of physical and emotional trauma because sometimes as a Christian body, we misunderstand God's role in these situations. We must have a clear understanding of exactly how God feels about His children, and that means we have to acknowledge certain lies that Satan will throw in our direction. Satan does not want us to believe that God cares for us or that God loves us. Satan desires for us to believe that God emotionlessly watched the traumatic experiences that have taken place in our lives. Many times, I hear the phrase, "God allowed it," from Christians. But I fear that we misuse that phrase as an excuse not to deal with some of the difficult things that happen within our human experiences.

Is God sovereign?

Absolutely. Sovereign means that God is ultimately in control of how things will turn out (Romans 8:28). Many times, however, we misinterpret this to mean that God is okay with people physically or verbally abusing His children, or that it was God's will for us to be hurt or damaged. That simply is not true.

If God is perfect, and His love for us is perfect, then we can determine that He does not have positive or apathetic feelings when evil things happen to us.

*"If you then, being evil, know how to give good gifts to your children, how much more will your Father who is in heaven give good things to those who ask Him." -*Matthew 7:11

This verse gives us a glimpse into God's care for us— He wants to give us good things. God uses the evil man in contrast with Himself to prove a very important point; God is holy and only gives us good gifts. It cannot be God's will for someone to attack, rape, assault, or belittle His children. With this in mind, it is important to consider why these evil things still happen to children of God.

Our Heavenly Father is all powerful, and it is true that He can prevent bad things from happening to us. So why doesn't He? We need to examine what it would mean for Him to stop evil from being perpetrated against His children.

I appreciate the fact that God has given me free will. It allows me to sincerely love and follow Him. If God prevented everyone from committing evil against His children, He would first have to take away their free will. The Lord allows everyone the privilege of free will, and unfortunately many people choose a sinful existence apart from Him.

When someone chooses not to follow God, they will inevitably do things that are against His Word. This does not mean that God wanted horrible things to happen to us as a result. Can God use difficult circumstances to expand our ability to minister to others if we let Him? Yes, of course.

"And we know that all things work together for good to those who love God, to those who are called according to His purpose." -Romans 8:28

God takes all the pieces of the lives of His children, positive and negative, and works them out according to His purposes. However, this scripture does not mean that God wants people to abuse you in the first place so He can work it into good later. Does God make beautiful things out of brokenness? Yes, He does, but the sinful behavior of others has to factor into situations of abuse and bullying.

If you have experienced physical or emotional abuse, please seek counsel. To admit that something horrible has happened to you does not mean that you doubt God (and if you do doubt God due to horrific circumstances, that is natural and you must work through those feelings with someone). God wants to help you through the healing process, and remind you how much He cares for you.

"The Lord is near to those who have a broken heart, and saves such as have a contrite spirit." -Psalm 34:18

"The sacrifices of God are a broken spirit, a broken and contrite heart— These, O God, you will not despise." -Psalm

51:17

In situations where there has been physical or emotional trauma, Satan will often remind you of what happened; he will feed you the lie that God must not sincerely love you if He allowed these things to take place. But don't believe Satan. God does love you! He never wanted you to be hurt, but we live in a world full of sin. God promises that if we trust Him to heal these wounds, He will comfort us and create something beautiful. When Israel was mourning because of their captivity in Babylon, God gave them this promise:

"To console those who mourn in Zion, to give them beauty for ashes, the oil of joy for mourning, the garment of praise for the spirit of heaviness; that they may be called trees of righteousness, the planting of the Lord, that He may be glorified." –Isaiah 61:3

Do you remember the process that Jesus went through before He was led to the cross? He was whipped, His beard was ripped out of His face, and He was spat on. He experienced extreme physical and emotional assault. I don't know all of the reasons that God allowed that to happen, but I do know that one of them was so that He could relate to you in your shame. He didn't have to experience shame in order to save us from our sins. All He had to do was die in our place. Yet, He went through traumatic abuse, and He did so willingly. In Isaiah 50: 6-10 we see how Jesus dealt with shame and injustice against Him.

"I gave My back to those who struck Me, And My cheeks to those who plucked out the beard; I did not hide My face from shame and spitting. 'For the Lord GOD will help Me; Therefore I will not be disgraced; Therefore I have set My face like a flint, And I know that I will not be ashamed. He is near who justifies Me; Who will contend with Me? Let us stand together. Who is My adversary? Let him come near Me. Surely the Lord GOD will help Me; Who is he who will condemn Me? Indeed they will all grow old like a garment;

The moth will eat them up. Who among you fears the LORD? Who obeys the voice of His Servant? Who walks in darkness and has no light? Let him trust in the name of the LORD And rely upon his God.'" –Isaiah 50:6-10

We see that Jesus trusted that God would deliver Jesus from any shame. From any disgrace. Where disgrace is, grace is there also.

If you have been sexually assaulted, experienced domestic abuse, or any other kind of assault or abuse (including verbal abuse), reach out for help. You cannot deal with it alone. You need the support of our Savior, and of a trusted friend, mentor, or counselor. There are several good books that deal with these topics, but don't turn solely to a book.

These are some suggestions for useful reading:

For anyone who has struggled with any kind of abuse or is supporting someone that survived abuse:
On the Threshold of Hope by Diane Mandt Langberg, Ph.D. (The workbook is also excellent)
For Sexual Abuse:
Rid of My Disgrace: Hope and Healing for Victims of Sexual Assault by Justin and Lindsey Holcomb
Counseling Survivors of Sexual Abuse by Diane Mandt Langberg, Ph.D.
Good News About Injustice by Gary A. Haugen
The Sexual Healing Journey by Wendy Maltz (This book is not from a Christian standpoint so she mentions some behaviors that the Bible mentions we should avoid. Make sure you keep that in mind when you are going through the book. The reason I include it in this list is because I have found that it is an invaluable resource.)

For Domestic Violence:
Is It My Fault?: Hope and Healing for Those Suffering Domestic Violence by Justin and Lindsey Holcomb
I have found all of these books to be illuminating and helpful in understanding God's role in our lives within the scope of trauma, shame, violence, and abuse. Remember to reach out to your church, a trusted friend, or counselor for further help.

CHAPTER 8

TO LOVE LIKE JESUS

When Jesus was on the Earth during His ministry, He did not find His personal value in being loved by others. Because of His confidence in God's love for Him, He was able to minister to others without any personal agenda: His love for them was truly unconditional. When we are in a relationship where we seek to feel loved ourselves, it puts pressure on the other person in such a way that they can never be sure that our love for them is actually unconditional. When we look for the love of others to give us personal value we are essentially sending a message to the other person that says, "I love you if you love me. It has to go both ways." That is not the message that Jesus Christ gives us, is it?

In Romans 5:8 it says, *"But God demonstrates His own love toward us, in that while we were still sinners, Christ died for us."* Jesus never said, "If you prove your love for Me, then I will save you." Jesus' love for us caused Him to give His life—He suffered on the cross, without any guarantee that we would love Him back. In the previous chapter we talked about how God was the one that risked His emotions by making the first move by adopting us as His children. If we follow His example, we should be willing to do the same thing. When we choose to become a living picture of the unconditional love of Jesus Christ, we can help others understand that there is a God who created this world, and that He loves them personally.

Before I understood God's love for me, I was not willing to risk the possible rejection associated with this kind of love. I never let people get too close to me. It was difficult to say, "I love you," to anyone outside of my family. As God changed my understanding about where my personal worth came from, it gave me the courage to be bold. I learned that if individual people rejected me, God would still love me.

I don't want to give you the impression that I think being rejected is fun. Rejection is painful, especially when you love others so openly and assure them of your care. There have definitely been times when my heart has been broken because the love I lavished on someone was not reciprocated. God has helped me through each season though, reminding me of His love and how He values and adores me. If I truly want to be like Jesus, I must be willing to risk repeated heartache.

The potential for pain is a possibility I choose to accept if it means that others have an opportunity to understand that the same unconditional love that God has shown me is also available to them.

"A new commandment I give to you, that you love one another; as I have loved you, that you also love one another. By this all will know that you are My disciples, if you have love for one another." -John 13:34-35

The verses above do not say, "weigh out the pros and cons of what could happen if you love someone and then decide if you should." It specifically addresses the love between believers, but it also tells us that the testimony of this love for others will identify us as followers of Jesus Christ. God won't force us to love this way. But, out of our love and appreciation for Him, we should follow His commands.

For a better picture of what self-sacrificing love looks like, I would encourage you to carefully study 1 Corinthians 13. There are numerous misconceptions about what love is, but this one chapter in the Bible should clear them up fairly quickly. We must remember the grace and mercy that God has lovingly given us and choose to give them to others. In the next section we will navigate through what 1 Corinthians 13 says about love.

* * *

LOVE, PRACTICAL APPLICATION

When I was a teenager, I was looking for someone to love me. I didn't understand that God loved me, and that God's love is more than enough love for any one person. I felt distanced from my family due to different circumstances, and the lack of love I felt led me to have difficulty saying "I love you," when people said it first to me. There was too much at risk. I became dramatically aware of this problem when one of my close friend's mothers told me she loved me before their family was getting ready to move away. I was so shocked that she said it (even though I had so desperately wanted to hear it) that I just stood there and said nothing. I remember thinking, "What is wrong with me? I'm supposed to be a Christian, an ambassador of Jesus' love, and I can't even tell this woman that I love her, too."

If you are self-conscious instead of God-esteemed, you will understand that saying "I love you," can be a potentially pain-filled phrase. Every time I said it, I was volunteering for rejection. Thoughts like *if they don't say it back I'll be mortified*, *they might stop being my friend if I say this*, and *I shouldn't make myself vulnerable* raced through my head constantly. I reserved these three words for family and a few select friends. I was not willing to risk anymore of my already dwindling confidence. No matter how much I wanted to show people the unconditional love of Christ, I wouldn't make myself be that open.

But, in the midsts of my journey to replace my deceitful pride with godly confidence, I realized that God's love and acceptance for me is all that I need. Because of this realization, I was able to learn to sacrifice my own feelings on His altar in a very open way. I realized that since I no longer looked to other people or myself to give my life value, that I wasn't risking anything I couldn't afford to risk. Do my feelings still get hurt? Of course, but now I don't see "I love you" as an opening for an eternal wound.

The purpose of love is to show someone that you care for them in such a way that nothing they do can change how you care for them. Earlier I said that I often tell my kids, "I may not always like the choices that you make, but I will always love you no matter what." This is the love that Jesus inspired by dying on the cross for our sins. He showed us His love by sacrificing His life.

How Can I Love Like Jesus Loves?
What does biblical love look like? So often, when love

is discussed, it is addressed as a feeling. And while I do believe we can feel love, that isn't always the case. Many times, love is a choice that we make. We decide to care for someone, no matter how they treat us. Everyone will point to 1 Corinthians 13 when you ask them about love because it is the best explanation of love this world has. It's not some cheesy poem about the feeling of being in love. This compelling chunk of scripture challenges us to do the most difficult thing any person can do: choose to love others in extremely difficult circumstances.

"Love suffers long and is kind; love does not envy; love does not parade itself; is not puffed up; does not behave rudely, does not seek its own, is not provoked, thinks no evil; does not rejoice in iniquity, but rejoices in truth; bears all things, believes all things, hopes all things, endures all things." –1 Corinthians 13:4-7

You may have these verses memorized. I did too, but I definitely didn't understand their various applications. I want to show you how selfless love really is, so I am going to give you examples of how each individual aspect of love applies to every person's life. But before we start, I want to remind you that God's Word has the power to transform both of our lives.

"Love suffers long and is kind"

Love causes us to put up with a lot of undeserved things. Even when people are mean, try to assassinate our characters, or try to punish us for things we didn't do, love tells us to be nice. Love instructs us to give grace and mercy to others over and over again. Love tells us to choose to suffer instead of letting everyone know that we are actually being wronged. Love tells us to let God be our defense.

"Love does not envy"

Love tells us to stay away from the danger that is

jealousy, and reminds us that if we do become jealous, we should rebuke ourselves and remember that God has already provided everything we need. A particular temptation we have is to become jealous over affection that is showed to other people, but not ourselves.

It is not righteous to be jealous of someone else that also has a relationship with a friend or family member. If you have a best friend that has been spending time with another person, rejoice in the fact that your good friend has another faithful friend. It is anti-productive to play games where we try to make sure that we get as much attention as someone else. This expectation will create unnecessary stress on our otherwise healthy relationships. Plus, if we look at jealousy all by itself, we realize it is selfish in origin. It is sin. "Jealousies" are listed under the works of the flesh in Galatians 5:19-21. Of course, this concept does not apply to a marriage situation in which one spouse prefers the company of a person who isn't the other spouse.

"Love does not parade itself"

True, self-sacrificing love does not cause us to go around saying how great we are. When Jesus was on the cross I don't remember Him saying, "I love you so much, I'm dying right now for your sins, aren't you so grateful for my love? My love is awesome." Although He could have said all of those things, and they would have been true, that isn't the example Jesus showed us while He was performing the ultimate act of sacrificial love. His love was and always will be humble.

"Is not puffed up"

True love and pride cannot coexist. Pride is sin, after all. Love doesn't tell us to think or say things like, "You're so lucky I'm doing this loving thing for you. You must be so blessed by my awesomeness."

"Does not behave rudely"

Listen very carefully, there is no biblical excuse for being rude. (I know, this one is hard for me, too.) No matter what is going on, self-control (a fruit of spirit) should be exhibited by believers at all times. Even when other kids are picking on my kid. Even when someone is unjustly accusing me of some sinful activity behind my back. No matter what is going on, being rude is not acceptable. We can be polite and still protect our kids. We can lovingly point out the truth if someone wants to debate with us, but let's not give into the temptation to be rude. It will ruin our witness as disciples of Jesus Christ every single time.

I'm not saying that I am never rude, I'm sure my younger brother would be quick to disagree with me if I did, but I try really hard not to be. And if I do give into temptation and adopt a rude attitude, I apologize and pray for God to help me repent quickly.

"Does not seek its own"

This tiny phrase of scripture is a gem. When you refuse to love someone because you are afraid of getting hurt, you are seeking your own. I have been guilty of this throughout my walk as a Christian. But, now that God has shown me the truth, I make every attempt to place my feelings in His hands. I choose to trust that He will take care of me when I obey Him by being vulnerable to rejection from others. When I say, "I love you," to a sister that needs encouragement, I don't expect her to reciprocate. If she doesn't say it back, it doesn't hurt my feelings. I am saying it because it is true, and God has commanded me to love others. Love does not consider its own feelings first, but always puts others ahead of itself. This is the kind of love that can transform the world. The biblical model we have of love seeks nothing in return for what it gives. That is what unconditional love looks like.

"Is not provoked"

This one is difficult. It means that when someone is actively trying to provoke us, make us angry, or push our buttons, that we refuse to give into our annoyance and instead keep on loving them. This is what Jesus was talking about when He said to turn the other cheek.

If someone is going to provoke and insult us, we shouldn't do the same thing in return, but let them continue with their insults. Self-control plays a huge role in our ability to keep calm when someone is hurling insults toward us. The fruits of the spirit often work in tandem, and in this case love is bolstered by self-control. Let's all pray for more self-control, a powerful fruit of the Holy Spirit.

We also need to have wisdom about when to remove ourselves from a bad situation. There are people in this world that annoy others simply to see if they can get an emotional response from the receiving party (some of us have behaved that way too). I have three children, so I get to see this unfortunate chain of events more often than not. It truly grieves my heart. I think God must feel the same way when He sees His children exhibiting this sinful and selfish behavior.

"Thinks no evil"

This tiny phrase means we refuse to sit around and think about how wrong someone else was, or what they deserve to get because of how they have treated us. Thinking no evil means that we actually refuse to let evil thoughts about that person wander around in our minds and fester. We all have thoughts that come into our heads. We are sinners, after all, living in a fallen world. But we can control what we allow to float around in our minds for minutes, hours, days, months, or years. Another great passage that deals with this issue can be found in Philippians 4:8.

"Does not rejoice in iniquity"

This section of Bible verse means two things. First, we must reject the temptation to rejoice in sin in general. Second, we must refuse to rejoice when bad things happen to other people (and no it doesn't matter what they have done to us in the past). Even if another person's current bad situation is a result of sin, real love has no reason to rejoice over it.

"But rejoices in the truth"

Love loves truth. God loves truth, so it is only natural that love would rejoice in truth. Even when the truth is hard to deal with, we need to rejoice that it is truth. We also see that when people practice biblical truth, there will be positive and exciting things that happen in their lives such as answers to prayer, fulfillment of prophecies, and other spiritual blessings, which are added reasons to rejoice[3].

"Bears all things"

Love helps us bear one another's burdens. Love can deal with any situation. Unconditional love means that you can still love someone even when they sin against you. We also know that in Matthew 11:29-30 Jesus said, *"Take My yoke upon you and learn from Me, for I am gentle and lowly in heart, and you will find rest for your souls. For My yoke is easy and My burden is light."* Jesus will teach us how to bring our burdens and the burdens of others and leave them at the cross, where we will find rest for our souls.

"Believes all things, Hopes all things"

These two go together. Love teaches us to believe that people can change, and that the transforming power of

---

[3] See Deuteronomy 5:33, John 8:12, and Psalm 128:1.

the love of Jesus Christ is accessible to anyone. Love wants us to say, "Yes, I believe that a serial killer can be born again." Love tells us to hope for the best. When everyone else says, "That person will never understand God's grace," love wants us to be the ones that say, "I hope that one day they will understand God's grace." Hope teaches us to respond to accusations in this manner, "Well, I understand you heard them say those nasty things about me, but until I talk to them one-on-one, I hope that they meant something more positive." Love encourages us to give others the benefit of the doubt. Love reminds us that our approach should be, "Innocent until proven guilty!"

"Endures all things"

Love helps us endure all things: not some things and not just things that people generally tolerate. Love can help us get through anything. Love tells us to leave our hurts and wounds at the cross with Jesus Christ. Love cheers us on, shouting "Endure! Persevere!"

THINGS LOVE DOESN'T DO

I want to be clear that even though through love we can be healed from any hurts and love means self-sacrifice and self-control, love does not mean you should actively let people harm you or your family. You can love someone without letting them be a ruling influence in your life (it is God's job to be that ruling influence). Not defending yourself doesn't mean that you allow someone to talk poorly about your spouse in front of you. It surely doesn't mean that you let someone demean your children. But, love deals with these problems maturely, and without anger. If someone wants to manipulate you, you can still love them from a distance without letting them cause you to sin. Love should never be used as an excuse to sin. Remember that as Christians we are told by Jesus Himself, *"Behold, I send you out as sheep in the midst of wolves. Therefore be wise as serpents and harmless as doves."* -Matthew 10:16

We have to be smart, but gentle. Sure we should speak the truth when people are lying, but the way we speak it is very important. We can say things in love, or in self-righteousness. Sometimes there isn't any other way to deal with a problem in love than to stay away from that person and pray. I have been in that situation before, and even though it was difficult, I knew that was the only righteous choice left. In those situations our game plan should be to pray and to hope, in love, that someday those hurts will heal. We should also pray that there will be repentance for any sin that has occurred.

WORTH THE RISK

As Christians, we are called to do all of the things mentioned in 1 Corinthians 13 for others, including our family members, spouses, children, and brothers and sisters in the fellowship. I'm not saying you should go around saying, "I love you," to everyone in your church. Be wise. If you are a woman, make sure you do not say this to man in a way that could be misconstrued and vise versa. In general, I don't say this to men. I let my husband be the one to say it. Likewise he doesn't say it to women, I do. There are people in our lives that do not understand God's love for them, and we are to be that picture of love in their lives. A simple, heartfelt "I love you" can go a long way in someone else's life.

Now, let's examine the specific benefits godly confidence has on our relationships.

CHAPTER 9

THE POWERFUL IMPACT OF GODLY CONFIDENCE

When you attain godly confidence, the way you behave and interact with others will change significantly. When you trust God, and believe that His love is what makes you special and valuable, you do not need human love to make you feel worthwhile. Remember that no other person can love you the way that God does. If you expect others to fulfill your need to be loved, you place an impossible expectation on them. Once you remove this expectation, your relationships will improve dramatically. In this chapter we are going to look at different types of relationships and examine how each type benefits from the security that comes from godly confidence.

❖ ❖ ❖

YOUR FAMILY

Relationships among family members can be extremely complicated. There is an automatic expectation of love, and when love is not reciprocated it creates unpleasant tension. We know that God commands us to love one another, but not everyone obeys God. Godly confidence impacts family relationships in two important ways. We are going to discuss them both, and I hope that whether you find yourself in one or both situations, that godly confidence will help you to break free from family-related emotional bondage.

The Search for Acceptance

As an adult, no amount of love or acceptance from your parents or other family members can satisfy the desire you have to be loved and accepted by God. This impossible expectation is unfair, and will stifle any chance of having healthy familial relationships. When you place your worth in the hands of another person instead of God, every disagreement between you and that person has the potential to turn into a life-defining conversation. In this situation, your value can disappear any moment if the other person chooses not to approve of your opinions or choices. In reality, if your family member disagrees with you, that is simply their opinion. God's word admonishes us to be respectful toward our parents and other family members. However, we do not need to let their opinions and wishes define our lives, especially if those opinions and wishes are unbiblical. The surety of God's love will naturally combat any unhealthy ideas or behaviors that appear in the lives of others around you. Embrace His love, and find the freedom to love dysfunctional family members who do not understand how their actions and choices have hurt you.

When Others Place Their Personal Value in My Hands

Godly confidence removes the pressure for you to fill the role of "worthiness giver" in the life of your family members because you realize that even if you wanted to, you couldn't be the one to give that other person's life value. Only God can do that. I am not saying that your family members will never place unrealistic expectations on you—I have several family members that crave love and attention from me in an unhealthy way. To me, this is evidence that they do not have godly confidence. They do not understand God's unconditional love for them, which grieves my heart heavily. On one hand, I do make repeated, special efforts to let them know how much I love them. On the other hand, I make sure not to encourage their unhealthy habits. If I love them the way God wants me to, I can't pretend that I can be everything that they need. Instead, I must point them to God.

There are special relationships that I know God has entrusted me with, like my marriage and my role as a mother, that are different than my other familial roles. For example, I spend a lot of time with my kids: I want to help them through life, to teach them about God, and to let them know in many different ways that I love them. However, this would not be something appropriate to transfer over into my relationships with other adults.

If I attempt to fill the need that another adult has to feel worth or know perfect love, I am setting them up

Kristin N. Spencer

for failure. Godly confidence helps me establish healthy boundaries with family members in order to nudge them closer to God. Remember that even though you are motivated by love to help family members, you cannot take the place of God in their lives. To attempt to do so will undoubtedly end in disaster because in essence you are acting as an idol. Anything we attempt to use as a replacement for God is an idol.

In some situations, it may be best to step out of the relationship for a time. This might be the case if a family member is being constantly confrontational and trying to provoke you to sinful behavior. If you feel like you may be involved in this type of situation, seek counsel from an older friend in the faith or your pastor.

I want to end this section on family by mentioning that only God is God. He alone provided His Son, who can provide the water of life that will cause us not to thirst ever again (John 4:14).

YOUR SPOUSE

The two principles that apply to family members also apply to your spouse. There is no way that you can completely fulfill them, and vice versa. No other human, including your spouse, will be able to give your life value and worth the way that God does. Only He can satisfy your desire to feel loved.

Unfortunately, many people accept the lie Satan perpetuates in worldly culture—if you can find romantic love you will be fulfilled. I used to accept this lie. For years, I was lonely in my marriage, grieving over the fact that even my husband's best attempt at love failed to meet my needs. My husband is awesome, and he loves me so much, but he isn't Jesus. He could never love me the way Jesus does. It is unfair to demand that from him because it is an impossible request.

Even though the last few years of our marriage have been much better, I didn't initially realize it was because I was starting to understand God's love for me. Since I have embraced the biblical concept of godly confidence, I have been able to enjoy my marriage in such a different way. Because of God's overflowing love for me, I am free to enjoy the love of my husband without the pressure of needing him to love me. I still want him to love me, of course, but I understand that his love for me is a bonus. It is like the extra level at the end of a video game. God's love for me is what defines my life, and the love my husband has for me is an additional blessing.

The opposite is also true. Now, I understand that the expectations I had for myself as a wife were unhealthy. There was no way I could fulfill my husband's desire to feel loved. Even though I was loving him the best way I could, I could never love him with a perfect love this side of Heaven. I cannot satisfy my husband's deepest desires, because I do not have the ability to do that. In fact, it's not my job. It is God's responsibility to do that, and my husband has to be willing for God to do it.

If you have noticed that your spouse doesn't understand how wholly and completely God loves them, there are a few things you can do. Pray for them. Pray, pray, pray! It is the most important and effective thing you can do. Fast and pray for them to gain this understanding. Point them to scriptures that show them God's love for them. Explain how God has grown your understanding in this area. Ask God to soften their hearts to His love.

One of the most important things you can do in your marriage is to open up dialogue and provide a safe, loving place for them to discuss their past hurts. Do not grow weary in doing good (Galatians 6:9), and continue to press into God. If your spouse sees your godly confidence, that may help them realize that they have neglected to be completely fulfilled by God's love.

* * *

YOUR FRIENDS

If you are confident in God's love for you, you will be a better friend. Something that often causes conflict in many friendships is that many companionships are based on unrealistic expectations. We have seen that in other relationships, this is damaging. The same is true for friendships. Your friends cannot satisfy your need for perfect love and acceptance—and the reverse is true as well. To love each other, encourage each other and minister to each other are all good and righteous things, but only God can give your life value. If we attempt to define ourselves by our friendships, we will be left feeling empty and frustrated. Satan knows how powerful godly friendships can be, and he wants to destroy them. I know many people that get angry or irritated if their friends do not communicate with them as often as they want; this is not loving behavior. If I am confident in the person God created me to be—in the fact that His love alone gives my life value—I will not get upset because a friend is too busy to email or to call me.

One of my closest friends is a very busy person. She has a family of her own, and various ministries in which she is involved. I only get a handful of emails from her each year, but I cherish each one. If she doesn't have time to respond to a prayer request I send her, I know she still prays for me. I love her and enjoy her company and conversation, but our relationship does not dictate whether I feel fulfilled or not. I know that I am loved by God, and that is what satisfies me; our friendship is an extra blessing. Would I be sad if she did not want to be my friend anymore? Of course! I would be devastated. But I would have to trust that God would be with me, heal my broken heart, and continue to sustain me with His perfect love. It is because of the confidence I have in God's love for me that I can be confident in my friendship with this amazing person. If I don't hear from her, I don't start to assume she is mad at me or has suddenly started to hate me. We understand that we love each other, even if we can't talk as often as we would like. Only under the umbrella of godly confidence is a friendship like this possible.

If you desire to have a blessed, God-centered friendship[4], remember that it is unfair for friends to expect one another to fill the role that only God can fill in our individual lives.

THE PEOPLE YOU MINISTER TO

Godly confidence and humility are attractive qualities to other people. Before I went through this journey, I never realized how much having godly confidence would impact my ability to be able to minister to others. Since I am no longer worried about personal acceptance or feeling loved, I am free to focus on other people's needs. Something else I have noticed is that people can tell if you follow the advice you give them. For example, when you tell them that God loves them and that should be enough, they watch to see if you are secure in His love. If I am writing a book about how to accept God's love and reject personal pride, then I should not

---

[4] In one of my other books, *You Can Do Better: Healthier, More God-Centered Relationships in 10 Easy Lessons*, I have outlined a biblically-based plan to achieve this type of friendship.

constantly comment about how much I hate my body. Since everyone is made to crave love, to experience being around someone who is fulfilled and confident intrigues people.

Before I understood the concept of godly confidence, I longed to be popular and accepted. What I failed to understand was that my insecurities were a deterrent to others wanting to spend time around me. Now people seem more drawn to me because of my confidence. I don't feel the need to make anyone accept or like me. I want them to see Jesus Christ in me, so I am loving and caring, but if they reject my attempts at friendship, I am honestly fine. I never thought I would be able to say that, but God has shown me the truth: His love and approval are truly all that I need. This is possible because I am God-esteemed.

Godly confidence does something else to create a powerful testimony. When we no longer care about how other people perceive us, we acquire the freedom to be completely transparent about our past sins and how God has delivered us from these sins. Transparency is one of the most important tools in ministry, because it touches people's hearts. If we are able to be completely honest about our sins, struggles, and victories, then God will be able to use our testimonies to help others. Our transparency creates a public account of His faithfulness to deliver His children out of difficult situations (in this case, us). Godly confidence has given me the ability to minister to others in a way that is more sincere and affective. It can do the same for you.

CHAPTER 10

CREATED EQUAL (EVERYONE FEELS INSECURE SOMETIMES)

I first started this project in 2014 as a personal guidebook for a seminar I taught at a women's ministry event in Athens, Greece. When my husband encouraged me to publish it, I didn't know what kind of a response a book like this would get. One of the many surprising things that happened was that I started to get emails from men asking me when I was going to come out with a less woman-centered version of this book. They told me that even though I was specifically addressing women, that the verses and instruction also helped them in their battles against insecurity.

After a lot of prayer and long conversations with my husband, we decided that instead of writing a book just for men who struggle with insecurity, I should rewrite *You Aren't Worthless: Unlock the Truth to Godly Confidence* to include both genders throughout. To close the book, I want to address men and women separately, because through this process, I realized there are incorrect stereotypes on both sides that need to be addressed. I hope that you will read both letters, as they hold vital information that will help you understand people of the opposite gender.

TO THE FELLAS

To my dear brothers in Christ, the first thing I want to say is that I see you. I know that you feel insecure sometimes, too. Confidence issues are not exclusive to women. I'm sorry that I left you out in the first edition of this book. Next, I want to say that I hear you. To everyone who wrote to me about how there is a need for a book that addresses insecurity in the lives of men, I applaud you for being so brave and transparent. I recognize that it isn't easy to share your struggles with a stranger. Thank you for trusting me with your words.

God's love is what gives you value. Whatever gender norms you feel trapped by, remember that the only standard to which you should aspire is the one set forth for us all in God's word. Having emotions doesn't mean you are any less of a man, but instead that you are conformed to the very image of God.

After watching my husband struggle through different seasons, I know that men have insecurities about body image and acceptance, just like women, and that men also have a whole list of other insecurities that women don't usually focus on. When Travis lost his job after our first daughter had skull reconstructive surgery, I noticed that his whole demeanor changed. It must be so hard to associate your worthiness of love with your ability to provide for your family. Though we are all called to work hard with what the Lord has given us, there will be seasons when circumstances outside of our control will dictate that we aren't able to do all that we desire for the people whom we love. Brothers, I encourage you to look to God, our heavenly provider, during those seasons.

During my marriage, I have often watched as God blessed my husband's hard work, but also how God provided for us when, despite everything Travis tried, we still struggled financially. God always came through, and I know He will come through for you. It isn't sinful to ask for help, but the sin associated with the pride-based decision to refuse to ask for or to accept help will act as a detriment to God's plan for your life. Remember, your worth is not based on how much money you bring home or how many hours you spend at work. Your worth is based on God's love for you.

Physical Appearance and Sexual Attraction

Earlier, when we discussed the temptation to allow our worthiness of love to be defined by our physical attractiveness, we focused mainly on one's physical appearance in relation to popular expectations of appearance from media. I know that for you men, your basis of attractiveness isn't based so much on your actual physical appearance, but instead it is based on whether or not you think others find you sexually attractive (i.e. whether people make sexual advances toward you).

Married Fellas

If you are married, this can be tricky, because women don't automatically associate the rejection of sexual advances, or total lack of sexual advances on their part, as a cause for feelings of insecurity. The best thing for you do if you are in this situation as a married man, is to describe to your wife the *feelings* you experience when this situation happens. Women are better at relating to feelings, instead of physical desires.

Single Fellas

If you are single, things are still tricky. As a holy vessel set aside for righteous works, you shouldn't be engaging in any behavior that has to do with lust (AKA fornication-themed desires). This means that you shouldn't want women making sexual advances toward you at all. The most important thing for you to remember is that your value as a person is not tied into how sexy women find you. If a woman is lusting after you, stay away from her! That is a dangerous situation, and no place for you to try to find personal fulfillment.

For more about this topic, Travis and I wrote a book called *Holy Sex Reboot: My Sexual Identity in Christ* for both single and married people who want to understand God's will for their sexuality.

The Urge to Fix

The last thing I want to touch on is that men have a natural urge to fix problems for the people they love. Though this natural tendency to want to fix is not inherently sinful, it can become sinful when you are trying to take God's place in someone else's life. God is the one who has ultimate control, and He allows problems to enter into our lives so we can grow in our faith of Him as He helps us through them. If there is a woman in your life who is exhibiting signs of lacking godly confidence, the best thing you can do for her is to communicate encouraging and appropriate words. If you feel God put it on your heart to help this woman, do so, but only then. The urge to fix her situation may cause you to choose behavior that leads to more harm than help. Allow the Holy Spirit to guide your words and actions.

TO THE LADIES

To my beloved sisters in Christ, you are precious and amazing. I hope that through the biblical truths I shared in this book that you are better able to understand what it means to have godly confidence. Before we conclude I just want to remind you of a few things we already discussed, while bringing up one last topic.

What Is the Truth in My Situation

In general, women relate to others based on emotional responses and motivations. Not all women experience this emotionally driven experience, as we follow a creative God, who has made all of us individual and unique.

When something happens, and we experience a feeling, before we respond we must ask ourselves this question, which sums up all of the questions we talked about in earlier chapters: what is the truth in my situation? Remember that if we try to find fulfillment in any other relationship apart from our relationships with Jesus Christ and God, our Heavenly Father, that we are asking another person to do the impossible. This can never end well. It is also equally important to remind ourselves that the standards for what is considered physically beautiful in this world are based on lies, which we are trying to avoid. There is no way we can live surrounded by the shell of godly confidence that will protect us from making choices based on sinful insecurities when we indulge in the continuous stream of lies that we find all around us. We must make choices to avoid the worldly things that tempt us to believe that we aren't wonderfully and fearfully made (Psalm 139:14). Let's make a pact not to go down the magazine aisle or watch certain TV shows or movies that encourage us to believe lies.

I don't know what your triggers are, but I know that there are certain things that make me feel worse about my physical appearance and I try to avoid them. When I feel insecure, I always do a mental evaluation. Was there anything in particular that kicked off those feelings, or was it just me indulging in sinful thoughts? Once I spend time trying to understand why I suddenly feel worthless, I can usually pinpoint the reason and avoid it in the future.

You Don't Like it When They Try To Fix Things

This last note is about how, as a woman, you can change your interaction with the men in your life to help them achieve godly confidence, and it's probably not in the way that you think. In the letter to the men I mentioned that women want them to listen when a problem arises. Remember that you don't like it when they try to fix everything *for* you without you asking for their help. In general, women are even worse about this because instead of trying to fix things *for* the men around them, they try to fix *the actual men.*

I want you to understand that this next statement has the potential to change your life: the men in your life do not need to be fixed by *you*. Yes, there are things that need to be fixed about all of us because we are all sinners. However, it is not our job to try to fix people.

There is one being that was expressly sent to Earth to do that: the Holy Spirit. Whenever we try to take the place of the Holy Spirit by instructing or demanding that someone change, we give the person a reason to ignore what the Holy Spirit wants them to do. Because of our attempt to play Holy Spirit, the other person feels justified in their anger, and ignores what God is trying to do in their lives. One of the things that men place the highest value on is respect, and when you approach them with a list of things they need to improve about themselves, you are not showing them respect. If you are truly concerned about a man in your life, pray for him to repent from his sin, find godly confidence through his reading the Bible, and know he is loved and uniquely made by God.

Chapter 11

FORGIVENESS AND HEALING

If you feel that the Holy Spirit is convicting you of a certain sin, whether it is pride, unforgiveness, or something else, the Bible shows that two steps must be taken for forgiveness and healing to take place. First let's look at forgiveness.

"If we confess our sins, He is faithful and just to forgive us our sins and to cleanse us from all unrighteousness." -1 John 1:9

But to whom should we confess our sins? In this verse it specifically speaks about the confession of our sins to our Heavenly Father. We can be sure of that because He is the only one that has the ability to forgive our sins. This is where true repentance begins. We tell God that we have sinned, and we are sorry. In turn, God receives our repentance and forgives us. It is a powerful moment that must be repeated over and over again in the life of every Christian. If we will do this, in return, God will cleanse us from all unrighteousness. I definitely need this type of cleansing in my life. But what about healing? Where does that come from?

Perhaps you have heard the common saying, "Talking about it helps." But did you know that this is a biblical concept?

"Confess your trespasses to one another, and pray for one another, that you may be healed. The effective, fervent prayer of a righteous man avails much." -James 5:16

It says right here in God's word that we should talk about our sins with a "righteous man." That doesn't mean that you walk around telling everyone the personal things going on in your life, but, if you want to have healing from sin, you should find someone that is trustworthy and righteous to share your sins with. Why? So that "you may be healed." These are God's instructions to us so that we might heal from our sins. We all sin. When people confess their sins to me I don't think, "Wow, they are so much more awful than I thought!" I usually think something like, "I know I'm capable of that sin as well." My heart is wicked and I know that. And when someone comes to me to confess, I get so excited! My elation isn't due to the sin, but because through confession they have started on the road to healing. I begin to pray for them specifically in an intercessory way. Through the process of confession, I have seen God work in the lives of many. I have also seen it happen in my life.

You can start down the path to forgiveness and healing today. Why wait? The shame and pain are not worth wasting your life on. Trust me.

CHAPTER 12

HOW TO COMBAT LOW-CONFIDENCE MOMENTS

ONE THING EVERY DAY

But how can you begin your journey to unlocking the truth to godly confidence? The best way to begin is to start at the origin of where all the lies and sin comes from: your thought life.

Make Your Brain Believe

The single most important battle you face each day is the war that wages within your mind. But don't take my word for it, check out what the Apostle Paul wrote to the Corinthians (they had a lot of the same issues then that we have today).

"But I beg you that when I am present I may not be bold with that confidence by which I intend to be bold against some, who think of us as if we walked according to the flesh. For though we walk in the flesh, we do not war according to the flesh. For the weapons of our warfare are not carnal but mighty in God for pulling down strongholds, casting down arguments and every high thing that exalts itself against the knowledge of God, bringing every thought into captivity to the obedience of Christ, and being ready to punish all disobedience when your obedience is fulfilled." -2 Corinthians 10:2-6

This is a perfect verse to end the book with, because it contains all of the themes we have been discussing. First, Paul talks about the confidence of the Corinthians. He tells them to be bold with confidence, because there are those that think we live and battle according to our flesh, the ability we have in our own strength. But the truth is that we don't live based on those limitations, because we don't use those weapons. Instead, we are "mighty in God for pulling down strongholds." The next part of the verse gives us the *how*. "For the weapons of warfare are not carnal ... casting down every high thing that exalts itself against the knowledge of God, bringing every thought into captivity to the obedience of Christ." In order to win the battle we are in, we must capture and crucify every thought. We must sort through each idea that floats into our minds through firing neurons and decided if they are righteous, or if they are sinful. The best defence we have against intruding thoughts is the truth of God's word.

In 2003, I was terrified to start university, so I wrote out Philippians 4:6 on a small piece of stationary and carried it around in my pocket each day. I would take it out whenever I felt nervous and it would remind me what the truth in my situation was. Then, when I first met Travis in 2005, I noticed there were Bible verses taped onto the walls of his room. He used them to wage his battle every day. When we lived in Greece I put up an extra folding chair on the wall (we used to hang our laundry on it because it was over a radiator) with Ephesians 4:1-3 written on it silver marker to remind us why we were in Athens. I know this method of mental spiritual warfare works because I have used it in my life to take over the battleground waged daily in my mind. I even have Micah 6:8 tattooed on my arm to remind myself what the Lord my God requires of me. You don't need to take it as far as a tattoo, but I promise if you put up the verses in the printable pack, read them everyday, and write them on your heart, you will be far better prepared for the daily battleground you will encounter. The best thing to combat low-confidence moments with will always be God's word. Check out the next section to find out how to use one trick every day to unlock the truth about godly confidence.

<u>One Thing Every Day</u>
There is one thing you can do every day to recover quickly from low-confidence moments. If this sounds too good to be true, I promise it is not. Understanding the truth about godly confidence isn't a guarantee that you will never have a low-confidence moment again. But, before I get to my proven approach for managing a low-confidence moment, I want to help you understand what a low-confidence moment is.

Have you ever been going about your day, working through your routine or relaxing, when suddenly you feel sad, depressed, lonely, or embarrassed? Your day had started out great and you were feeling awesome, but now you want to clear your schedule go back to bed. What happened?

Each memory or conversation has the potential to trigger a low-confidence moment. That may sound like an overwhelming fact, but understanding how triggers are associated with your thoughts and interactions will help you deal with and avoid low-confidence moments.

For example, let's say you have a cousin that always makes rude comments about your teeth. Every time you see him, he brings up braces, telling you that if you're going to keep smiling, you need to make a well-needed investment in symmetry. What a jerk. Because of his unkind actions, every time you even hear about him, you feel ashamed of the appearance of your teeth. The idea of your cousin triggers a low-confidence moment. Rude Cousin's behaviors have made everything about him a trigger for you.

This is a sequence of events that illustrates how all low-confidence moments work. A thought or interaction triggers uncomfortable feelings. Many times we don't even realize that a trigger is what has caused a low-confidence moment. We trudge through the rest our day, feeling lousy and not understanding why we feel that way.

<u>Recognize and Deal With the Trigger</u>

Once I realize that I am experiencing a low-confidence moment (and sometimes it takes me a while), there is a list of steps I mentally run through that helps me recognize and deal with my emotions in a healthy way. If you use this list every time you realize you have entered into a low-confidence moment, you will unlock the truth to godly confidence and transform your everyday life.

Step 1: Pinpoint the origin of the uncomfortable

feelings (AKA your trigger).

Step 2: Try to understand the lie that this trigger tempts you to believe.

Step 3: Combat the lie with scripture.

Step 4: Remember that you are God-esteemed.

Step 1 usually takes me the longest because the origin of my low-confidence moment has snuck its way into otherwise healthy thoughts. Remember, our enemy is sneaky. Satan doesn't want you to realize where your negative feelings come from because then you can deal with them in an emotionally healthy way. Christians who are emotionally healthy are far more effective at advancing God's Kingdom than emotionally unhealthy Christians.

Let's go through all four steps using the example of our tooth "expert" cousin, Rudy (see what I did there). I'll pretend that he's been bothering me about my teeth again.

Step 1: Pinpoint the origin of the uncomfortable feelings (AKA your trigger).

My dad tells me that Rudy is going to be in Western Pennsylvania and he's wondering if he can stay at my house for a few days so he doesn't have to pay for a hotel. Lovely. The rest of the day I feel grumpy, and I can't stop running my tongue over my teeth. What's the origin or trigger that's causing my low-confidence moment? Rudy himself. When a person has repeatedly made you feel less-than, they become the actual trigger.

Step 2: Try to understand the lie that this trigger tempts you to believe.

In this case, the specific lie that the trigger (Rudy himself) tempts me to believe because of one my physical traits—my less than perfectly aligned teeth—means that I am visually repugnant. The first lie here is that my physical traits define whether or not I'm worthy of love. We know that isn't true. But we also know that God doesn't make mistakes when He creates us. We have to live according to God's standards, not the world's standards. When it comes to how you should look, the two opinions vary wildly. Rudy is trying to impose the world's standards of appearance on you, but as a child of God you are free from those impossible expectations. This is the second lie.

There's nothing wrong with me straightening my teeth, but I can't expect that to change the way I feel. If I base my worthiness of love on my physical appearance, I will always be left feeling empty and less-than. That brings us to the final step.

Step 3: Combat the lie with scripture.

What lies do I need to combat with scripture? The first lie that my physical traits define whether or not I'm worthy of love and acceptance. The idea that we have to live up to the world's expectations of physical appearance is the second lie. Every time you experience a low-confidence moment you need to battle against it with truth. This is a long war, but we can win one battle at a time, each and every day. As we win more and more battles, they become easier to win and we expend less effort to maintain our godly confidence. But how do we do battle? We remember God's Word. So, what scriptures can I use to combat the lies that Rudy's trigger unleashed on my mind? Here are a few I have memorized to help me do battle when it comes to insecurities related to my physical appearance:

"For we are His workmanship, created in Christ Jesus for good works, which God prepared beforehand that we should walk in them." -Ephesians 2:10

"Do not let your adornment be merely outward—arranging the hair, wearing gold, or putting on fine apparel—rather let it be the hidden person of the heart, with the incorruptible beauty of a gentle and quiet spirit, which is very precious in the sight of God." -1 Peter 3:1-3

"For the Lord does not see as man sees; for man looks at the outward appearance, but the Lord looks at the heart." -1 Samuel 16:7

Step 4: Remember that you are God-esteemed

It is so important to remember where your esteem comes from. You were bought at a price. As a child of God, you have been adopted. You are chosen and loved. Don't let anyone or anything cause you to forget that.

Because I know that memorizing these four steps along with verse memorization can seem a little daunting, I have compiled a list of each Bible verse quoted in this book organized by the chapter in which it appears. You can find this quick list in the section labeled "Bonus Material," and also as a part of a packet of printables you can download for free by signing up for my newsletter. Along with this list, the printable packet you get for joining my newsletter contains print versions of the daily steps and a collection of Bible verses I have made and photographed for you to print and put up around your house. I have also included card-sized printables among your free packet that are perfect for on-the-go encouragement. Put them in your wallet or purse and hang up the larger ones in your room.

You've got this. Now that you know how to combat

low-confidence moments, which will go a long way to helping you unlock the truth godly confidence, make sure to keep reading. The 30-Day Challenge will also help you on your journey.

To receive your free printable packet, go to:
youarentworthlessbook.com/packet

30-DAY CHALLENGE

I Can't Do This Alone

When we decide to make important changes, we often need extra motivation to keep us going. Is there anyone in your life that can help keep you accountable? In order to help you and your accountability partner start off on the same page, I've created free resources that will give your friend all of the information they need to help you on your journey. Just go to: YAWquickstart.com

There you will find a free download of the first three chapters of this book in PDF form, my Confidence Analysis Quiz so that your friend can determine where they are on the confidence scale, a ten-minute quick start audio guide (for those with limited time), and a thirty-minute explanation of the main principles that I have written about in this book. These are things I offer to help make sure you can get the accountability you need without the need to purchase anything. I hope you and your accountability buddy find these resources helpful.

Getting Started

Now that you have a better understanding of how godly confidence works, you can take your printables and start a 30-Day Challenge to Godly Confidence. But you don't have to do it alone. You are more than welcome to join our Facebook Support Group:

You Aren't Worthless :: Confidence Support Group
https://www.facebook.com/groups/341719280051669/

On our Facebook Group you can go to the pinned post and find a link to download the 30-Day Challenge to Godly Confidence PDF to print. In the meantime, here are the instructions you need to start and finish your journey to godly confidence as you work your way, one day at a time, toward your goal of understanding that you are God-esteemed.

Every Day
Remember these steps from the previous pages:

Step 1: Pinpoint the origin of the uncomfortable feelings (AKA your trigger).
Step 2: Try to understand the lie that this trigger tempts you to believe.
Step 3: Combat the lie with scripture.
Step 4: Remember that you are God-esteemed.

Week 1: Establishing Your Toolkit
Throughout this book, you have been given several tools to use when you recognize a thought that goes against what God says about you in the Bible. But now you need to do a practical breakdown of all the ways you can battle against the unattainable goals that the world sets for you as an individual. Though no one is perfect, it is important to remember that you are loved, cherished, and God-esteemed.

Take your printable and place the different verses where you can see them. If you like frames, go ahead and frame them. Otherwise, you can use something like double stick tape, or white wall putty to stick them up in areas throughout your dwelling where you will see them multiple times per day. When you see them, make an effort to read them out loud or in your mind. Try to memorize them so that you can use them later to ward off a low-confidence moment. Take the card-sized printables and put a few in your wallet or purse. Take them out when you have a few minutes free and work on memorizing them then. In fact, when you have a low-confidence moment and you're out, you can use the cards to ground yourself and to focus your thinking on the truth. Use these verses and phrases to meditate on God's Word. These are important tools that you don't want to be without.

Practical Steps:
-Spend 15 minutes every day in memorization.
-Make a note of how many low-confidence moments you have each day, and then at the end of week 1 add them together and divide that number by seven. You now have an average of how many low-confidence moments you have each day. Don't be daunted by the number even if it seems like there are too many to count. Now you need to set a goal of how many low-confidence moments you would like to see in a day. Even though I have been doing this for years, I rarely have a zero low-confidence moment day. If zero seems impossible right now, pick a number that seems more reasonable. Talk to your accountability person about your future goal. We will talk about how to achieve this goal in the coming weeks.
-Acknowledge your hard work to take the first steps in changing your low-confidence moments into God-esteemed recognition moments. You

have been working hard.

Week 2: Make Your Brain Believe

The verse for this week has already been part of your memorization routine, but now you need to make your brain believe that what it says is true. Read through it with me again.

"...God, who cannot lie..." –Titus 1:2

God cannot lie, and that means that every one of those verses that you've been memorizing is true. You are loved by a Creator and Heavenly Father. You were made for good works which are promised to be completed within your lifetime.

"For we are His workmanship, created in Christ Jesus for good works, which God prepared beforehand that we should walk in them." –Ephesians 2:10

Practical Steps:

This week, instead of working solely on memorization, I want you to think through each verse. As you see the verses around your house and when you pull out the printable cards, take each one through this thought pattern:

–Why is this verse true?

–What does this verse communicate about me specifically?

–What about God's character reflects this verse? Then take some time each day to do your own research to answer these questions.

–What other verses (examples in the Bible) can I find that prove this verse is true?

–Is there a Bible character that also had a hard time believing this verse was true for them? What happened to them because of this particular insecurity?

Week 3: Write It Down

This week you will focus on writing for fifteen minutes at the beginning of the day, and fifteen minutes at the end of the day. Writing not only helps you understand things you might not think (many people discover things they didn't know about themselves through journaling), but it also reinforces ideas and will help with your verse memorization.

You will find it helpful to go through these different entries with your accountability person. If you feel self-conscious about sharing, remember that you chose that person carefully because you can trust them.

Practical Steps:

Morning Reflections
Read through the four steps of how to deal with a low-confidence moment again.

Step 1: Pinpoint the origin of the uncomfortable feelings (AKA your trigger).
Step 2: Try to understand the lie that this trigger tempts you to believe.
Step 3: Combat the lie with scripture.
Step 4: Remember that you are God-esteemed.

What to write: Try to make predictions about what triggers you might encounter based on the triggers you've been discovering since the challenge began.

Evening Reflections
Think about your day and look at your

predictions from the morning reflections in your journal.

What to write: Were any of your predictions right? If yes, how can you continue to use the truth in the verses and the steps to better deal with your triggers? Were any of them wrong? Take a minute and reflect on your successes. You have made the decision to believe God's Word and it's really changing the way you think.

At the end of each day, take time to meditate on this verse:
"And do not be conformed to this world, but be transformed by the renewing of your mind, that you may prove what is that good and acceptable and perfect will of God." –Romans 12:2

Week 4: Hearing from God
   The most important aspect of staying grounded to the truth and understand that you are God-esteemed, valued because you are part of the family of God, is spending time with Him every day. This week you are going to focus on reading your Bible. If you already do that, great. If not, now is a great time to start.
   It is also important to communicate with God through prayer, so that will also be a focus this week.

Practical Steps:
–Spend 10 minutes each day reading through the Bible. If you don't have an idea of where to start, I recommend 1 John. It's all about God's love for you.

-Spend 5 more minutes journaling about what God has shown you through the verses you just read. It doesn't have to be long. One sentence will do.

-Spend 10 to 30 minutes praying. It doesn't need to be fancy, just tell God how you're feeling, all that He means to you (praise), and ask Him for guidance for the future. You can also pray for the people around you. This is a really great practice because it takes the focus off yourself, and after all this thinking about your worth and your feelings, that can be needed and rewarding.

-Talk to your accountability partner (or share in the group) about some of the things God is showing you through the Bible and your prayer time.

You've Made It!

You can continue the steps from week four indefinitely, and make sure to go through the mental checklist of steps for each low-confidence moment you face. But by now, if you've followed through each week, you should see a huge difference in your approach to godly confidence.

Make sure to check out the group. We'd love to hear about your struggles and successes.

I NEVER THOUGHT...

I never thought I would be the right person to write a book like this; it still surprises me. When I first rededicated my life to Jesus, I knew that one day I would want to help others understand how radically Jesus changed my life—I never imagined it would be through a book (I also didn't realize this would be the first of many books I would write). If God is able to deliver me from personal pride and feelings of worthlessness, I know that He can do the same for anyone. God will never give up on trying to help you understand how deep His love for you is. I hope this book has been as much of a blessing for you to read as it has been for me to write. I pray that you would understand how these truths can transform your walk with God. I love you very much and I will continue to pray for you. I know that God has amazing plans for your life, and I pray that you will embrace them as you embrace Him! God bless you.

"For You formed my inward parts; You covered me in my mother's womb. I will praise You, for I am fearfully and wonderfully made; Marvelous are Your works, and that my soul knows very well. My frame was not hidden from You, when I was made in secret, and skillfully wrought in the lowest parts of the earth. Your eyes saw my substance, being yet unformed. And in Your book they all were written, the days fashioned for me, when as yet there were none of them. How precious also are Your thoughts to me, O God! How great is the sum of them. If I should count them, they would be more in number than the sand; when I awake, I am still with You." -Psalm 139:13-18

If you found this book helpful, please consider leaving a review on the platform where you purchased it. Reviews are absolutely vital for authors and don't need to be long. All you have to do is write one or two short sentences, or even words, about what you thought of the book overall. Thank you so much for all of your support.

Chapter 13

BONUS MATERIAL

BIBLE VERSE QUICK LIST

Chapter 3
> Genesis 1:27
> 1 John 4:18

Chapter 4
> *On Pride*
> Proverbs 16:18
> 1 John 2:16

Proverbs 11:2
Proverbs 13:10
Proverbs 14:3
Proverbs 16:5
Proverbs 16:18
Proverbs 29:23
1 Timothy 3:6
Isaiah 14:12–14
1 Peter 3:1–3
1 Samuel 16:7

On Humility
Titus 3:1–2
Proverbs 3:34
Proverbs 15:33
Psalm 25:9
Psalm 34:2
Proverbs 11:2
Proverbs 29:23
1 Peter 5:5
Timothy 2:23–26
Matthew 18:15–17
Matthew 5:38–39
Philippians 2:8
James 3:14–18

Chapter 5
On Self-Hatred
Colossians 2:8
Ephesians 5:29
Ephesians 2:5

On Self-Esteem
    Proverbs 3:19
    Psalm 16:11
    Galatians 5:19-24

On Ignoring Insecurities
    Exodus Chapters 3-4
    Judges Chapter 6
    Titus 1:2
    Hebrews 4:6
    1 Corinthians 3:11

Chapter 6
    John 4:6-18
    Genesis 1:27
    1 John 3:1
    Ephesians 2:4-7
    James 1:18
    2 Corinthians 11:2
    Jeremiah 31:13
    1 John 4:18
    Ephesians 2:10
    Psalm 139:14-17
    Matthew 10:30
    Psalm 56:8
    Genesis 15:5
    Romans 5:8
    2 Timothy 1:8-10
    John 3:16
    Philippians 4:8

Kristin N. Spencer

Proverbs 20:29
Romans 8:13
Matthew 7:13-14

Chapter 7
Ephesians 6:4
Job 1:18
Exodus 34:6-7
Psalm 109:16
Corinthians 12:10
Philippians 1:6
Ephesians 2:4-5
Ephesians 4:31-32
John 1:12
1 John 4:19
1 John 3:1-2
Romans 6:23
John 17:23-24
Ephesians 1:4
Psalm 68:5-6
Matthew 7:9-11
1 John 5:14-15
Luke 12:27-31
Jude 24-25
Psalm 111:10
1 Corinthians 13:7
Matthew 7:11
Romans 8:28
Psalm 51:17
Isaiah 61:3
Isaiah 50:6-10

BIBLIOGRAPHY

Bibliography

[1] "Pride" Def. 1. Merriam Webster Online, Merriam Webster, n.d. Web. 26 Feb. 2015. DICT dictionary.

[2] "Greek Lexicon :: G5012 (NKJV)." Blue Letter Bible. Web. 3 Mar. 2015. <http://www.blueletterbible.org/lang/lexicon/lexicon.cfm?strongs=G5012&t=NKJV>.

[3] "Hate" Def. 1. Merriam Webster Online, Merriam Webster, n.d. Web 6 Mar. 2015.

[4] Rosenberg, Morris. "Determinants of Self-Esteem." Society and the Adolescent Self-Image. Citation Classics, 13 Mar. 1989. Web. 26 Feb. 2015. <http://garfield.library.upenn.edu/classics1989/A1989T475800001.pdf>.

[5] Branden, Nathaniel. The Power of Self-Esteem. Deerfield Beach, Flo.: Health Communications, 1992. 8. Print.

ACKNOWLEDGEMENTS

Acknowledgements

Since this is an updated edition, I feel like I should update the acknowledgements.

Thank you...

Travis, Ksena, Kati, and Timo for letting me sneak off during our road trip to work on the new sections and edits as they came back.

Lise Cartwright my coach and teacher about all things marketing. You are the best!

Mom (LeAnn Coletta) for watching the kids play in the pool so that I could have a couple of hours each day to work on this project while we were in California along with your support and positive attitude.

Sarah Papajohn and Rachel Secor for proofing the original version and all of your feedback.

Maria Mountokalaki, my trusted editor, for polishing my FINAL manuscript until it shone (check out literarysymmetry.com for Maria's awesome services).

My Relaunch Team: Autumn, Elizabeth, Desiree, Rinda, Zulema, Debbie, Ash, Veronica, Lisa, Fiaz, Debbie M., Doretta, Lena, Karen, Katie, James, Melanie, Brooke, Mardelle, Tammy, Jennifer, Michelle, Debbie C., Tom, Breanna, Lindsey, Amy, Debra, and Ann.

My mom, Peggy, for all of your support and cheerleading.

Aunt Ellen for your constant encouragement and support.

My dad, Brian, for your love and understanding.

Aunt Sherry for your love and encouragement and

faith in my writing.

Brandon, Flora, and Brandy. Love you guys so much!

Denise Murphy for your frank conversations when I was working on this.

To the Greensburg Writers Group, you are all so motivating and I count myself lucky to be including in your diverse collective.

For Dad (Allen/Pappou)... I miss you every day. I will never forget your words of encouragement. When I feel like a failure I hear your words of affirmation and I remember that they were a reflection of God's love.

Most of all, Jesus Christ and my Heavenly Father. Thanks be to God for all He has done and will do with a broken vessel such as myself.

ABOUT THE AUTHOR

Kristin N. Spencer spends part of each day imagining up new worlds and beings when she isn't busy taking care of her three children and writing partner husband T. E. Spencer. When she's not writing you can find her working in full time ministry, sewing cosplay costumes, or watching geekesque movies. She writes whatever genre she wants including but not limited to Non-Fiction, Contemporary Fiction, Sci-Fi, Space Fantasy, and traditional Fantasy. Kristin studied Comparative World Literature at California State University, Long Beach and received a Bachelors, which she fondly calls a degree in reading. Her favorite movie is Sabrina (the Julia Ormond version) and her favorite person is Jesus.

She has worked in full time ministry for the last eight years, and also runs the women's discipleship website *Sincerely Adorned*.

OTHER BOOKS BY AUTHOR

Christian Nonfiction
You Can Do Better: Healthier, More God-centered Relationships in 10 Easy Lessons
Holy Sex Reboot: My Sexual Identity in Christ (coauthored by T.E. Spencer)
Confident Nobody: Finding Fulfillment in Your Right-Now (*Coming 1/12/2020*)

Fiction
The Desires and Decisions Series
(Middle Grade to YA)
Newfangled
Flummoxed
Kerfuffle

The Plunge Into Darkness Series
(Recommended age: 16+)
Plunge Into Darkness
The Knotted Woman (*Coming April 2020*)
The Chorus of the Fallen (*Coming May 2020*)

<u>Your Free Confidence Quiz</u>

Maybe after everything you've read, you wonder where your starting point is as far as godly confidence. Well, don't worry. I have a handy quiz you can take that will let you know where you're at. What the best part? That it's totally free. Go get yours now at: youarentworthlessbook.com/free

In addition to your free quiz, you will also get fun email updates and more free stuff. I hope you check it out.

Are you interested in improving all of your relationships in as little as ten days?

You Can Do Better: Healthier, More-God Centered Relationships in 10 Easy Lessons

comes out on October 13th, 2019. You will find a sample below. To sign up for release day and presale information, please go to: kristinnspencer.com/youcandobetter

Choose *Love*...

"Love suffers long and is kind; love does not envy; love does not parade itself, is not puffed up; does not behave rudely, does not seek its own, is not provoked, thinks no evil; does not rejoice in iniquity, but rejoices in the truth; bears all things, believes all things, hopes all things, endures all things." -1 Corinthians 13:4-7

Love is precious. There is nothing else like it, and this is especially true when we think about the love of God. Because of how valuable love is, we often think of it as something that we should distribute with caution, measuring out each drop against the amount that has first been given to us. The problem with that way of thinking is that it puts a lot of pressure on our relationships. In fact, that model of love distribution is unbiblical. Love is precious, yes, but we are not limited in how much love God gives us. The love that comes from the Father is unlimited. The verse with which 1 John 4:8 ends is, "God is love." If we realize how infinite God is, we realize that His love is also infinite. God is the source of love.

When we look at love as something to be traded instead of freely given, we become confused about God's plan for love. In 1 Corinthians 13:5, we see that "love does not seek its own." When we only give love in exchange for receiving love, that is exactly what we do, seek our own. Choosing love is a risk. It hurts when we love someone and they don't show us that same love in return. It makes us feel rejected and worthless. But didn't God warn us that would happen? Verses like Luke 10:16 and John 15:18 remind us that when people reject us, they are rejecting Christ, and that if the world hates us we need to remember that they hated Jesus first. Our flesh, the opposite of our spirit, gets angry with us when we love. Have you ever noticed that it feels so much better to hate and become bitter? Think about the last time someone disagreed with you about something you really cared about. Did their actions in that moment make you want to love them more? Probably not. In fact, you might have felt angry and rejected. Those natural feelings, which lead to hatred, are a result of our living in a fallen world. God never encourages hatred. Our Heavenly Father has chosen us as His children. He doesn't want us to wallow in human rejection, when He has paid such a high price to welcome us back into fellowship with Him.

Often, when we hear that something bad has happened to a person that was mean to or betrayed us, we feel happy. We also see in today's verse that, "love does not rejoice in iniquity." Whether our betrayer is dealing with the consequences or their own sin, or that of someone else's, we should never allow ourselves to rejoice or feel happy when sin happens. We must remember that love "bears all things," which means it is our duty as followers of God to listen to and empathize with others when they experience difficulties. And when we listen, we ought to hear, and not to form some sort of argument with whatever that person says.

It is also important to recognize when a relationship has become abusive. In those circumstances we should put distance between ourselves and the abusive person, but that doesn't mean we should stop loving them. We can still pray for them, while we remove ourselves from that abusive person's destructive influence.

Ponder this: How would our actions change if we trusted God to refill any love we passed out, instead of waiting for people to reciprocate (show love back)? What would the church as a body look like if we all chose to love this way? How can this choice affect our witness as we share the gospel with non-believers?

Prayer Time

Take a few minutes and ask the Lord if there are relationships in your life where you could love in a more generous way. Ask Him to fill you with His love, so that you can give it to others. Pray for Him to help you have wisdom to know how each person in your life needs to be loved by you. Remember that you can always ask God for more love and for comfort when you feel rejected or hated by someone.